CONTEMPORARY CHRISTIAN STUDIES
EDITOR: PAUL AVIS

THE ADEQUACY OF CHRISTIAN ETHICS

THE ADEQUACY
OF
CHRISTIAN ETHICS

BRIAN HEBBLETHWAITE

MARSHALL MORGAN & SCOTT

Marshall Morgan & Scott
1 Bath Street, London EC1V 9LB

First published by Marshall Morgan & Scott 1981

ISBN 0 551 00919 5

Phototypeset by Input Typesetting Ltd, London SW19 8DR
Printed in Great Britain by
Biddles Ltd, Guildford, Surrey

Contents

Preface

For a long time it was believed that morality without religion was impossible. Atheists were thought inevitably wicked. Christianity was held to reveal the true nature of goodness and to make it possible for men and women to lead upright lives. Now the tables have been turned. Secular moral philosophers not only defend and explain morality without religion. Many of them criticise Christian ethics, including the teaching of Jesus, on moral grounds. This book is an attempt to consider seriously these objections to Christian moral teaching, to trace them back to certain major themes in eighteenth and nineteenth century philosophy, and to distinguish for discussion the main lines of criticism advanced by twentieth century moralists. A number of writers and movements in modern Christian ethics are surveyed, in order to discover how far they lay themselves open to these criticisms and how far they succeed in repudiating them. Some consideration is then given to alternative religious moralities, commended in the other religions of the world, and also to other aspects of religion and life than the purely ethical. But the adequacy of Christian ethics consists not only in its capacity to meet objections, but far more in the positive ideal of individual and common life which it sets before mankind, and in the spiritual resources which it holds to be given to men and women for the realisation of that ideal. The book ends, therefore, with a positive sketch of what a specifically Christian ethic might be.

CHAPTER ONE

Criticisms of Christian Ethics since the Enlightenment

It is a striking feature of Christian ethics in modern times how much Christians have been thrown on the defensive. Not only their doctrines, but also their fundamental values, attitudes and ideals, have been subjected to criticism. Moreover the criticism that really bites is moral criticism, objections, on moral grounds, both to Christian beliefs and to Christian ideals. The problem is not just the way in which, as a matter of fact, Christians have fallen short of their ideals. It is the ideals themselves that have been thought to be inadequate.

There have, of course, been many different criticisms of Christian ethics. But there have also been many different versions of Christian ethics, and it is often hard to pin down precisely what it is that is being attacked. The target constantly shifts. It often happens that a Christian moralist will allow that a specific criticism is justified as far as it goes, but will go on to say that the critic must have an inadequate or debased version of Christian ethics in mind. The true version is held to escape unscathed. Thus criticisms of Christian otherworldliness are met by references to the doctrine of Creation; criticisms of Christian individualism are met by references to the social gospel; and criticisms of the authoritarian nature of Christian ethics are met by reference to the freedom

9

of the Christian man and his discovery of his own true nature in relation to the God who made him. Even criticisms of the fountainhead of Christian ethics – the teaching of Jesus – are met by a barrage of differing interpretations of what he really meant.

Many of these criticisms are now made from within the Churches. We have learned to be self-critical in respect of Christian moral teaching, just as we have in respect of doctrinal and biblical teaching. Thus Don Cupitt, in his book, *Crisis of Moral Authority*,[1] endorses many of the external criticisms of Christian moral attitudes and adds several of his own, before recommending a radical purging and reconstruction of Christian ethics on the basis of the teaching of Jesus. And the German theologian, Dorothee Sölle, in a book entitled, *Suffering*,[2] roundly castigates the Christian tradition for encouraging sado-masochistic attitudes to God and man, before she proceeds to recommend a radical theology of social action. Hers is only one of many books now appearing which recommend such a radical theology of liberation and this-worldly 'praxis' – to use the fashionable term – and it is well known how deeply such ways of reconstructing Christian ethics have come to dominate the thinking of the Secretariat of the World Council of Churches. But we are bound to ask ourselves about the adequacy of these versions of Christian ethics. Are they genuinely Christian? Can they really claim to represent an authentically Christian stance in the world?

So we have a double problem. Not only do we have to ask ourselves about the adequacy of Christian ethical teaching, pinpointing an undistorted core of peculiarly Christian ethics and investigating its ability to withstand criticism. We have also to ask ourselves whether any suggested presentation of Christian ethics actually succeeds in expressing the essence of

10

Christian morality. In other words any version of Christian ethics has to defend itself on two fronts. It has to make out its claim to be Christian, and it has to make out its claim to be moral, indeed to be more adequately moral than any rival view.

My emphasis in this book is on the latter task. We are to look at moral criticisms of Christian ethics, and at the ability of Christian ethics to resist those criticisms. But we have to keep an eye on the other problem. We must ask ourselves whether the Christian ethics which, in answer to criticism, we expound and defend is genuinely Christian.

Before embarking on our main task, I must say something about the *basis* of moral criticism of Christian ethics. The question will, no doubt, already have arisen in the minds at least of Christian readers. On what basis are people judging Christian ethics? Where do they get the moral standpoint from which to criticise Christian moral teaching? Do not Christians claim to speak of the will of God and of the commandments of God? On what grounds can human beings criticise those? Why should any notice be taken of such presumption? The answer, it seems to me, is this: we have come increasingly to recognise that many different and conflicting things are asserted, at different times and in different traditions, both within and outside Christianity, to be God's will. We have come to recognise that no assertion of what is or is not God's will escapes the human, fallible and relative nature of all men's utterances. Bertrand Russell made this point, amusingly, when he observed that the supposedly radical views of Tom Paine, the eighteenth century author of *The Rights of Man*, could now be safely uttered by any archbishop. So we can never be absolutely sure, even within the Christian tradition, that we have rightly grasped what is the will of

11

God. But there is a second factor to be reckoned with as well. We have also come to recognise the phenomena of human goodness, conscience and the moral sense, however partially distorted, in all religious contexts and in non-religious contexts too. This combination of factors, the diversity and relativity of religious views of what is God's will and the undoubted fact of goodness and conscience outside Christianity or even religion, has led us to suppose that no one set of moral views can place itself beyond criticism.

This problem has come to be admitted even in respect of biblical faith. We cannot, morally speaking, defend the alleged command of God to Abraham to slay his son, even if it was only a test; we cannot defend the injunction to massacre the Amalekites; we cannot defend the treatment allegedly meeted out to Ananias and Sapphira in Acts chapter five. All these morally repulsive elements in the tradition of biblical faith are rejected today on moral grounds by Christians and non-Christians alike. This seems to be true, even if we find ourselves going on to say that, properly understood, Christian morality enhances natural morality and indeed corrects it, where its moral vision is partial or distorted. The fact remains that it is often so-called natural morality that has awakened Christians to the need to purify their own moral vision and to reject the primitive and morally repulsive forms in which it has sometimes expressed itself.

How is the Christian moral theologian to understand this state of affairs? A preliminary answer might go something like this: Christians certainly believe that all goodness stems from God and reflects both God's own nature and His will for man. But recognition of this comes in two ways: the good for man is built into human nature and can be discerned, however fragmentarily and incompletely, in what makes for human relationship and human flourishing. This 'natural' recognition of the good can be affirmed despite the 'fallen' state of man. But the true good for man is further revealed, so Christians believe, through the saving acts of God, culminating in the story of Jesus and his Resurrection. Here too there is no guarantee of freedom from distortion in the human media of revelation or in man's understanding of divine revelation. So it is quite possible for the two channels of moral knowledge, human experience of goodness and human response to the revelatory acts of God, mutually to illuminate and correct each other. Moral criticism of religious revelation-claims is possible because natural human morality is itself a reflection of the image of God in man. Christian morality's criticism and enhancement of natural human morality are possible since they reflect the definitive revelation of God's nature and will through His saving acts. But the two channels, on this view, cannot be ultimately incompatible, since it is the same divine nature that is reflected, however hazily, in human goodness, as is reflected most clearly, on the Christian view, in the character of Christ. But the divine revelation, including the character of Christ, has itself to be understood and applied correctly by men and women down the ages; they may get it wrong, and thus be open to moral criticism.

That, as I say, is a very provisional and preliminary answer to the question why Christians should take moral criticism of their ethics seriously.

It is worth noting that similar problems arose in ancient Greece, long before the birth of Christianity. In Plato's dialogue, the *Euthyphro*, the participants discuss whether piety is what the gods love, or whether the gods love something because it is pious anyway. The Euthyphro dilemma, as it is called, is rephrased nowadays as the question: is something good because God commands it, or does God command it because it is good? The dilemma seems insoluble. Either goodness is arbitrarily what God commands, so that if God commanded something monstrous, say torture, that would be, by definition, good, or goodness is what it is independently of God – He commands something which is good already – in which case the moralist need not bring Him into the picture. But it has been pointed out that the Euthyphro dilemma is soluble after all.[3] We have only to recognise that human goodness is real and there to be both commended and commanded by God, but that human goodness itself reflects the essential goodness of God. God is its ultimate source and goal. It is not arbitrary but rather the very nature of God to command the good; and goodness in man is the very image of God in creation. Thus, again, there are two mutually correcting and mutually enhancing sources of knowledge of the good – human nature as God created it, and God's revelation of himself. Each provides the basis for criticism of our idea of the other.

Whatever we may think of these preliminary reflections, the fact of moral criticism of Christian ethics cannot be denied. I shall be concentrating on some of the forms it has taken since that great upheaval of Western thought and culture which we call the Enlightenment. In this chapter I shall pick out four of the leading figures of eighteenth and early nineteenth thought, turning in the next chapter to certain nineteenth and early twentieth century critics, in particular, Nietzsche, Marx and Freud. In the third chapter, I shall examine a number of recent and contemporary twentieth century critics of Christian ethics.

Let us begin by looking at two of the central figures in the history of modern Western philosophy – David Hume (1711–1776) and Immanuel Kant (1724–1804). Just as these writers

14

present enormous threats to the possibility of Christian metaphysics, so they present, in very different ways, powerful challenges to the adequacy of Christian ethics. It is not that the philosophy of the Enlightenment was, in general, hostile to religion or to a religious morality. Kant, indeed, to all intents and purposes identified religion and morality and claimed to be setting forth the true moral content of Christianity in his book, *Religion within the Limits of Reason Alone* (1793). Hume, along with some of the French 'philosophes', was rather exceptional in his criticisms of religion and of Christianity in particular. Yet even his moral philosophy was not wholly alien to Christian ethics. It has much in common with the characteristic moral philosophy of the eighteenth century British moralists, many of whom, like Francis Hutcheson (the chief inspirer of Hume's moral philosophy, according to Norman Kemp Smith[4]), retained a basically Christian framework for their ideas.

Nevertheless, Hume based his interpretation of morality on an analysis of human nature, and particularly on the sentiments of approval and disapproval which we all have towards human actions, our own and other people's. Morality was not a rational affair. No 'ought' could be derived from an 'is', whether that 'is' be an empirical fact or an alleged transcendent one. Nothing moral follows from the alleged fact that 'God is our Creator', according to Hume. Morality follows rather from our dislike of pain, our sympathy for others, our feelings of benevolence.

It is easy to see how this account of morals could be detached from any religious context, and also how it could form the basis of an attack on dogmatic, intolerant and authoritarian forms of religious morality. It is true that in his essay on 'Superstition and Enthusiasm' Hume claims to be attacking

15

primitive religious attitudes or distortions of true religion. But he attacks 'the narrow implacable spirit of the Jews'; he explicitly links monotheism with intolerance; he attacks the monkish virtues of mortification and passive suffering; and it is clear from his *History of England* (1754 ff.) that he thought the Roman Catholic Church to be guilty of superstition and the Protestant Churches to be guilty of enthusiasm.

Hume's antipathy to the Christian religion is therefore clear. He was not, however, a dogmatic and aggressive atheist. His contemporaries speak of him as an easy-going, benevolent and tolerant man. He thought that we remain on safe ground when we stick to common human nature, in matters both of belief and morals. He was as sceptical about exaggerated philosophical beliefs as he was about religious ones. It is true that attitudes of tolerance, mitigated scepticism and benevolence are not incompatible with Christian ethics, and Hume was on friendly terms with many of the liberal and moderate clergy of his day. But it is clear that he thought intolerance and fanaticism to be much more characteristic of religion, and, not surprisingly, he met with much opposition from the more dogmatic clergy of the Scottish church.

In what sense then does Hume represent a challenge to the adequacy of Christian ethics? In two ways, I think. Firstly his analysis of morality, in terms simply of feelings of approval and disapproval, if it were itself an adequate account, would make a religious basis for morals redundant. And secondly, he points to regrettable consequences of religion in history – intolerance, superstition, inhumane enthusiasm and bigotry.

A reply to Hume, therefore, would have to show, first, that moral values cannot be accounted for solely in terms of human feelings and in fact require a religious basis. It would have to show, secondly, that the instances of fanaticism and cruelty which Hume deplores are in no sense inevitable consequences of religion, but rather its very opposite – and indeed equally to be deplored from a religious point of view. In the third place, it would have to show the positive illumination and moral creativity which a specifically Christian ethic can provide. These are some of the tasks which will be undertaken in chapters four and five below.

Kant's challenge is a much more insidious one. He, as I pointed out, is claiming to uphold the moral law embodied in historical Christianity properly understood. In *Religion within the Limits of Reason Alone*, with remarkable ingenuity, he makes every doctrine of the Christian Church, as well the example of Christ himself, illustrate his own philosophical understanding of the supreme principle of morality, as he had expounded it in earlier books. It is well known how, for Kant, morality is not imposed on us from outside. On the contrary, the moral law or categorical imperative, as Kant calls it, is a law of our own rational nature. It is imposed upon us, quite autonomously, from within. All that matters – and it matters unconditionally – is the good will, according to which I act only on those maxims which I can rationally will to be a universal law and according to which every human being is to be treated as an end in himself and never as a means only.

Since, for Kant, morality is a matter of reason, the historical elements in Christianity are quite superfluous. Nor is God required as a ground of the moral law. That, according to Kant, would be to turn morality into a heteronomous affair and deprive it of its transparent rationality. (A 'heteronomous' ethic is one which holds that morality is a matter of duties imposed on us from outside by the will of another – in this case, God.) Admittedly Kant does postulate God as the guarantor of the possibility of the eventual coincidence of goodness

17

and happiness (since, clearly, in this life they do not coincide), but he emphatically does not postulate God as the ground of moral value. It is our own moral reason that prescribes the basic form of our duties categorically. Consequently Kant holds that whatever is good in religion is theoretically derivable from moral reason itself. Hence his opposition to rituals and dogmas. Christianity, in its beliefs and ethical teaching, must rather be shown to embody the categorical imperative. It is not surprising that the Prussian King thought *Religion within the Limits of Reason Alone* to be a dangerously subversive book, even though Kant himself claimed to be interpreting, not criticising Christianity.

The Prussian King's reaction is not surprising because it is indeed the case that Kant's firm defence of the autonomy of morals and his belief that our own moral rationality yielded the criteria of right and wrong set morality above religion and provided a basis, not only for moral criticism of the aberrations of religion, but also for the reduction of religion to the status of, at best, an embodiment of the moral law. Moreover, in so far as a religion such as Christianity insists on speaking literally of the will or nature of God as the foundation of ethics, it was shown up as thoroughly inadequate in failing to bring out the autonomy of morals.

This insistence on the autonomy of morals, this emancipation of morality from religion, is the chief point in which the philosophy of the Enlightenment represents a threat to the adequacy of Christian ethics. It undermined the very basis of Christian ethics' claim to higher insight and universal validity. This, clearly, goes much further than just providing grounds for the moral criticism of distorted Christian teaching.

It is instructive to compare Hume and Kant at this point.

In a curious way, Hume's moral philosophy, for all his hostility to Christianity, was less of a threat to the adequacy of Christian ethics than Kant's moral philosophy, for all his claim to be sympathetic to Christianity, properly understood. Hume's moral philosophy was certainly subjectivist and non-cognitive, but the moral sentiments on which it rested *could* be viewed as implanted by God, as indeed they were viewed by many of the British moralists with whom Hume had much in common. But Kant's moral philosophy was avowedly opposed to any form of heteronomy. To seek to ground the good will on something outside itself was to cease to be talking of morality at all, according to Kant. Thus the autonomy of morals involves an outright and radical denial of the adequacy of any heteronomous religious ethic.

Once this step had been taken, the path was open to much more fundamental attacks on the adequacy of Christian ethics than anything one finds in Hume, whose own attacks *could* always be regarded simply as attacks on aberrations and distortions of the real thing, and not on Christianity and religion as such.

The more radical Kantian dissatisfaction with the very basis of any heteronomous ethic was taken further by two of Kant's successors, in the school which we know as 'German Idealism'.

Johann Gottlieb Fichte (1762–1814) was greatly influenced by Kant. In many ways he was an austere and 'religious' man; but in 1799 he was expelled from his professorship at Jena for teaching atheism. This was the famous 'Battle over Atheism' (Atheismusstreit); but it is arguable whether his views were really atheistic. Like Kant's, Fichte's moral philosophy was an ethic of conscience and the good will rather than obedience to divine command. His first book, *Critique of all*

Revelation (1792), was published anonymously and at first thought to be by Kant himself. Its title already indicates Fichte's hostility to religion's claim to authority in faith and morals. But Fichte was much more explicit in his rejection of the idea of personality or self-consciousness in God. He certainly taught that the finite proceeds from the infinite and is transcended by it, but for Fichte, personality is in essence a finite notion. Hence the impossibility of the very notion of an infinite sovereign will. These were the views at issue in the Atheismusstreit, and Fichte's objections to the notion of infinite personal being have been very influential down to the present day, even among philosophers far removed from German Idealism, who argue along similar lines against the meaningfulness of the notion of an infinite person. The theologian Wolfhart Pannenberg regards Fichte's objections to personality in God as one of the most telling criticisms ever made and as demanding a full answer from the systematic theologian.[5] Again it is clear that this sort of criticism is much more penetrating than a series of objections to particular practices and ideas, supposedly resulting from a religious or Christian view of the world.

The philosophical development of the young Hegel (Georg Wilhelm Friedrich Hegel, 1770–1831) is also very interesting for the student of those ideas which came to be held to undermine the very basis of a religious ethic. A collection of Hegel's early writing has been published under the English title, *Early Theological Writings*,[6] but, as Walter Kaufmann points out, these would better be called 'anti-theological writings';[7] for they are very critical of all 'positive' religion, by which Hegel means religion which simply 'posits' dogmatically certain so-called truths of faith and morals. At first Hegel too was influenced by Kant and in his short life of Jesus gives

20

us a completely Kantian Jesus, teaching nothing but the moral law within. But soon Hegel became dissatisfied with Kant. Even a self-imposed moral law he held to be dehumanising, and in 'The Positivity of the Christian Religion' and 'The Spirit of Christianity and its Fate' he taught rather a Christianity of freedom and love, a religion that had somehow got overlaid in Christian tradition by 'positive' dogmatic teaching. But, for our purposes, we need to note how, in the interests of his ideal of the free spirit, Hegel came to criticise the notion of an objective sovereign God over against us. In 'The Positivity of the Christian Religion', he says 'The doctrine of God's objectivity is a counterpart to the corruption and slavery of man', and he goes on to suggest that, having objectified a transcendent God in this way, men proceeded to fight, murder and denounce each other on his behalf. Hegel's criticism, then, of Christian ethics is not that it has, as a matter of fact, led to the horrors of religious wars, but that it was bound to have these consequences, once God was thought of as objective, transcendent, sovereign will.

However, according to Hegel, this conception of God was a corruption or distortion of the true Christianity, which he describes in 'The Spirit of Christianity and its Fate' as an immanent spirit of love. To quote him: 'Faith in the divine is only possible if in the believer himself there is a divine element which rediscovers itself, its own nature, in that on which it believes . . .' In fact he goes so far as to say 'only a modification of the Godhead can know the Godhead.' We observe how far Hegel goes from orthodox Christianity in order to rescue Christianity.

This brief examination of four leading figures from the eighteenth century Enlightenment has shown how far-reaching was the effect in the ethical sphere of these men's new-found confidence in their own freedom and autonomy. Once an independent basis for moral judgement had been acquired, whether it was understood in terms of human moral senti- ments or of human moral reason, it became only too easy, as well as quite obviously correct, to criticise the authoritarian, intolerant and aggressive Church of the Middle Ages and the Renaissance. The Inquisition, the wars of religion, the sev- enteenth century witch-hunts, were all, quite obviously, mor- ally repulsive. But the critique, as we have seen, went much further than that. Such criticisms, in themselves, could be and were shared by enlightened Christians of the eighteenth century. They could reasonably claim that Christian ethics itself required such criticisms to be made. But, with Kant and his followers, a new and much more serious threat begins to emerge. The very idea of a sovereign will over against us comes to be thought of as ethically damaging and destructive of true morality. On such a view, Christian ethics, however reformed, could never be adequate. Containing within itself an irreducible element of heteronomy, it necessarily condemns itself at the bar of moral reason.

How might the defender of Christian ethics reply to all this? Along the lines of our preliminary sketch of the relation between Christian and secular ethics, he would have to try to show that the discovery of a basis for moral judgement in human nature and the human situation can itself be regarded as a providential gift, whereby the corruptions and contradic- tions of religion can be pointed out and rectified. But in three ways he will want to counter-attack and reject the more ex- treme thesis of the wholly autonomous nature of morality. In the first place, he will need to show how insecure a purely autonomous ethic is, that, as a matter of historical fact, secular ethics, deprived of the support of a transcendental source of

22

value, has not been able to sustain the high moral seriousness of Kant and Fichte. In the next chapter, we shall be looking at a more alarming instance, in Nietzsche, of man's independent moral autonomy. Then, secondly, he will need to show that the essence of morality is not lost, but rather enhanced and secured when the good human will is seen to reflect and realise a sovereign will, which is itself absolute goodness and the source of our own being. And thirdly the defender of Christian ethics will need to show how secular morality is itself subject to corruption and contradiction and in need of criticism in the light of the love of God. These points will be developed as we proceed to consider further examples of attacks on the adequacy of Christian ethics, and to examine some attempts by Christian moral theologians to describe the ethical core of the Christian vision.

NOTES

1. London: Lutterworth, 1972.
2. English trans., London: Darton, Longman and Todd, 1975.
3. See H. Meynell, 'The Euthyphro Dilemma', in *Aristotelian Society Supplementary Volume 46* (1972), and also J. L. Mackie, *Ethics* (Harmondsworth: Penguin Books, 1977), pp. 229–232.
4. *The Philosophy of David Hume* (London: Macmillan, 1941).
5. See 'Types of Atheism and their Theological Significance' in *Basic Questions in Theology*, volume 2 (English trans., London: SCM Press, 1971).
6. G. W. F. Hegel, *Early Theological Writings* (English trans., University of Chicago Press, 1948).
7. See 'The Young Hegel and Religion' in *From Shakespeare to Existentialism* (New York: Beacon Press, 1959).

CHAPTER TWO

Nietzsche, Marx and Freud

It is commonplace among French and German students of history of ideas that Nietzsche, Marx and Freud are the three most significant makers of the modern world. The inclusion of Nietzsche in this list may surprise British and American readers. To the Anglo-Saxon mind, especially, Nietzsche is too bizarre a figure to be taken seriously. Marx and Freud, it will be agreed, have had a pervasive influence on the twentieth century, but, if a third major figure is to be identified, it is more likely to be Darwin than Nietzsche. Yet Nietzsche was undoubtedly a major *prophet* of the modern world, and it is worth considering him along with Marx and Freud; for, if these three writers have one thing in common, it is uncompromising hostility to religion, in particular to Christianity – and that predominantly on moral grounds.

Friedrich Nietzsche (1844–1900) was the son of a Lutheran pastor. After abandoning theology, he became first a classical scholar, and was made Professor of Classical Philology at Basel at the age of twenty-four. But already wider influences had made their mark on his thinking, in particular the philosophy of Arthur Schopenhauer (1788–1860) and the music dramas of Richard Wagner (1813–1883), whose monumental genius and creativity fascinated the young Nietzsche. Nietzsche's first book, *The Birth of Tragedy* (1872), introduces the notion of a 'Dionysian' tendency in Greek art – by contrast with the 'sweetness and light' traditionally found there – the Dionysian element of frenzy and passion, reckoned with in Greek tragedy, but suppressed, so Nietzsche claims, by Socrates and Plato. This becomes one of the 'Leitmotifs' of his own thought. The idea that 'the goal of humanity cannot lie in the end but only in its highest specimens' is to be found in his next writing which cover the period of his famous break with Wagner over Wagner's nationalism, antisemitism and espousal, in 'Parsifal', of the ideal of the simple fool. The 'will to power' only gradually acquires a central place in Nietzsche's thought, though it can be found in the collection of aphorisms, published under the title, *Human, all too Human* (1878). But it is *Thus Spake Zarathustra* (1883 ff.) which contains the bulk of his most characteristic notions: the death of God, the emergence of the Superman (Übermensch) to overcome the nihilism which will inevitably follow God's disappearance from the scene, and the theme of eternal recurrence – the cyclical view that everything returns again and again in the same configurations. The later works on morals spell out Nietzsche's contrast between master and slave moralities, and repeat the thesis that decadence and nihilism can only be overcome in an elite who embrace a higher culture and a higher morality. Nietzsche himself became an increasingly isolated figure and was insane for the last ten years of his life.[1]

I suggested that Nietzsche was more of a prophet than a maker of the modern world, and there is no doubt that he had an astonishing perception of the way things were going intellectually, culturally and politically. He spoke of himself as 'untimely', aware of that to which other people were blind and would be blind for a generation. This is exemplified in the famous passage on the death of God in *Joyful Wisdom* (*Fröhliche Wissenschaft*, 1882), in which the madman goes

25

into the market place in the morning hours with a burning lantern, announcing that we have murdered God – the greatest deed ever done – and that churches now can be only the tombs and sepulchres of God. The listeners are silent and stare at the madman in astonishment. He throws his lantern to the ground and says, 'I came too early . . . This tremendous event is still on its way . . . the light of the stars requires time, deeds require time, even after they are done, before they can be seen and heard. This deed is still more distant than the most distant stars, and yet (men) have done it themselves.' Nietzsche's parable brings out the seriousness of the fact of the death of God in the minds of men. Elsewhere he fulminates against the views of those who complacently drop the idea of God and think they can go on as before. Christianity is a system. 'By breaking one main concept out of it, the faith in God, one breaks the whole . . .' he says in *The Twilight of the Idols* (1888). Morality too cannot remain the same. The logical consequence of the death of God is nihilism. Nineteenth century writers were quite wrong to think that ethics could remain the same without the framework of religion. On the contrary, if God is dead, nothing is true; all is permitted. This is not of course Nietzsche's own position; it is his insight into what happens when a world loses its meaning. There is plenty of evidence to confirm his prophecy.

He also prophesied ideological wars, western decadence, mass culture creating a new barbarism, the atrophy of education brought about by the fragmentation of knowledge. Many passages have an uncanny accuracy and quite lack the bizarre quality of the death of God parable – for example his denunciation in *Joyful Wisdom* of the way in which he saw the Americans breathlessly striving for money, abandoning calm reflection, courtesy and leisure. This passage shows something of the positive side of Nietzsche. In fact it is a mistake to think of Nietzsche as an immoralist. He undoubtedly rejected traditional morality, including Christian morality, but far from accepting the nihilism which he saw following from the death of God, he wanted to set against it a positive new morality, the elitist vision of the Superman, the man of spirit and passion and culture, embodying the will to power and all the excellence of which humanity was capable. It has been suggested that a combination of Napoleon and Goethe would meet his specification! But this was not just a response to the threat of nihilism. Nietzsche's 'transvaluation of values' involved an independent attack on traditional morality and the concept of God, irrespective of his dramatic reporting of the death of God. He saw both traditional morality and religion as a morality of the herd, a decadent and crippling affair, fundamentally destructive of life and spirit. In *Ecce Homo* (written in 1888), he says, 'Morality is the idiosyncrasy of decadents, actuated by a desire to avenge themselves upon life.' Christianity in particular he sees as deliberately repressing spirit and passion and encouraging self-renunciation and the cult of the weak and feeble. His polemic against Christianity is in fact extended to socialism and democracy as well – all of them being, for Nietzsche, expressions of a slave morality, of the resentment of the many against the few.

Curiously, he distinguishes between the Christian ethic and the ethic of Jesus. But he rejects both. Implausibly he makes Jesus out to be a kind of Dostoevskian idiot figure. He respects such a man; but still rejects him (as he did Parsifal) in favour of the individual whose affirmation of life takes the form of the will to power. And so in *The Antichrist* (1888) he sets the figure of Dionysus against that of Christ.

Nietzsche's individual ideal and rejection of what he calls

27

the morality of the herd sets him very much against the socialist morality of Karl Marx. But he shares with Marx a pronounced debt to the left-wing Hegelian philosopher, Ludwig Feuerbach (1804–1872). Feuerbach had urged the replacement of theology by anthropology; for the concept of God, on his view, was a self-projection of man upon the heavens. Men should rather strive to realise their own true humanity. We shall see how Marx applied this teaching to man's economic and social life. Nietzsche, by contrast, sees God as an obstacle to passion and individuality, to the self-assertion of the exceptional individual. Nietzsche is to be contrasted with Fichte too. He was not just rejecting a personal God. He denied God and the transcendent altogether in order to make room for man's own freedom and creation of value. In this we can, after all, detect the *influence* of Nietzsche on twentieth century thought. For this is the source of the atheistic existentialism of Jean-Paul Sartre[2] – and indeed Nietzsche's style and emphasis on subjectivity have been very influential on the development of existentialism generally.

In the face of Nietzsche's sustained polemic against Christianity and Christian ethics, it is surprising to find Christian apologists ready to espouse the cause of Nietzsche. Yet such there are. Werner Pelz, for instance, tells us that he has sold his copies of Barth and reads only Nietzsche. In his own books,[3] Pelz embraces the exuberance and passion of Nietzsche as expressing the essence of the Christian vision. One can see what he means: after all it was Nietzsche who said, 'We do not easily negate; we make it a point of honour to be affirmers.' It was Nietzsche who said, 'Light feet are the first attribute of divinity'. One can appreciate his denunciation of the enemies of life. One can even see what he meant by saying that he took it as a definition of truth that whatever was said by a priest was false. But there are limits to the chameleon-like ability of Christian moralists to wriggle out of criticism and reappear in a new guise. I take it that the apologist for Christian ethics, aware of Nietzsche's contempt for the weak and espousal of elitism and individual self-affirmation, will see in Nietzsche an undoubted adversary.

Another theologian who makes positive use of Nietzsche is Alistair Kee, who, in *The Way of Transcendence*,[4] accepts the death of God as an unquestionable cultural fact in the modern world. But Kee at least recognises that Nietzsche's own response to this situation – the cultivation of an elite morality for Supermen – is not, by any stretch of the imagination, a possible version of Christian ethics. Kee accepts the atheistic framework, but commends a vision of life for others as a positive ideal, which he calls, 'the way of transcendence', and regards as modelled on the human figure of Jesus.

I do not think, however, that it is enough simply to set an ideal of compassion and life for others over against Nietzsche's ideal of the Superman, and hope that it will turn out more attractive. The defender of Christian ethics is bound to go much further than that and attack not only Nietzsche's analysis of Christian ethics as decadent and life-denying, but also his view of God as a threat to life and freedom.

What we shall look for in the sequel are expositions of Christian ethics in which human life is understood to find its true fulfilment in relation not only to one's fellow men but to the God who made us for himself, the God in whom we live and move and have our being. We must look for a profounder sense of what it is to be life-affirming, an interpretation of what Jesus meant by saying, 'I am come that they may have life and have it more abundantly', a proper grasp of the true freedom of a Christian man, and an understanding of the individual and social sense of finding life through losing it. But the point I wish to stress here is that we can only meet the threat of Nietzsche and his atheistic existentialist successors if we can show that God is not a threat to freedom, but the very source of a meaningful freedom. As Heidegger saw,[5] only a more radical inquiry into being can overcome Nietzsche's metaphysic of the will. For the theologian (though not for Heidegger) this means a more radical enquiry into the infinite being in whom we find our true being, and, conversely, a demonstration of the self-defeating nature of the self-affirmation of the human will. The tables can be turned on Nietzsche only when God is seen as the very condition of the possibility of true freedom.

But this defence against Nietzsche cannot take place solely within the framework of his individualist approach; for the expositor of a viable Christian ethic has also to take account of the far more influential and powerful social critique of Marxism.

Karl Marx (1818–1883) was known as a left-wing Hegelian and an atheist even as a student. In his earliest writings he holds that 'criticism of religion is the foundation of all criticism'. These early writings are now conveniently collected together in the Penguin Marx Library under the title, *Karl Marx: Early Writings*.[6] They contain a sustained polemic, based on Feuerbach's analysis of religion as a human projection, against the religious element in Hegel's writings on the state. But for Marx, the projections of religion are a phenomenon of alienated consciousness. They freeze men in a state of self-alienation. Marx criticises Feuerbach for treating man as an abstract individual rather than as a product of society, and for failing to realise that the religious sentiment is a social product, reflecting a particular form of economic and social structure, in which the majority of men are alienated from the product of their labour and thus from their true selves.

So Marx goes beyond Feuerbach in his treatment of religion. It is not simply to be dissolved into its human essence. For religion, Marx writes in 1843, in an essay on the Jewish question, is the heart's cry of alienated, atomised man. Consequently the opposition between Jew and Christian will only be overcome when religion is abolished and both find their true human selves in a properly structured society.

Marx's most celebrated onslaught on religion comes in 'A Contribution to the Critique of Hegel's Philosophy of Right' (1844). It should be pointed out that, by now, Marx is saying that the business of philosophy is not so much criticism of religion as criticism and indeed transformation of the world of social relations, which is reflected in the illusory halo of religion. For the burden of Marx's argument is that men's oppressed condition gives rise to religion as justification and consolation for their suffering, but only at the level of fantasy. Religion is both an expression of and protest against real suffering. It is 'the sigh of the oppressed creature, the heart of a heartless world and the soul of soulless conditions. It is the opium of the people'. Man must throw off his chains and then the need for this illusory consolation will disappear. This view of religion as part of the ideological superstructure reflecting the real infrastructure of alienated economic relations in society remained with Marx throughout his life and writings. Clearly his criticism of religion is part and parcel of his moral criticism of the unjust social and economic structure that it supposedly reflects.

Marx's criticism, then, like Nietzsche's, is basically moral criticism. But it can be argued that Marx's criticism is less overtly hostile than that of Nietzsche, just because of Marx's

31

sympathy for the alienated masses. Religious values are a consolation to the oppressed. They are illusory, because man has it in him to change the alienating economic and social system, and by becoming socialist man to render religion otiose. But the values in this ideal of socialist man are more powerful and compelling – and of course closer to Christian values themselves – than those of Nietzsche. They are the ideal of 'from each according to his ability to each according to his need'. Nietzsche's ideal of the Superman, the outstanding individual who affirms his will against, or rather above, the resentful herd, is in the nature of the case a morality for the few. Correlatively, Nietzsche's view of Christian ethics was much more hostile than that of Marx. For Nietzsche, Christian morality expressed the resentment of the weak against the strong. Both writers see the source of real value in man himself – to that extent both are disciples of Feuerbach – but only Marx can seriously be called a humanist in ethics. This is why he represents the much more formidable and plausible challenge to Christian ethics.

Subsequent Marxist criticism of Christian ethics has become sharper and more overtly hostile. This is because attention has turned from the consolatory function of religion for the alienated masses to the use of religion by the oppressors to justify the status quo. The moral force of this aspect of Marxist criticism has been admitted and illustrated by the American writer on Christian ethics, Reinhold Niebuhr, whose views we shall be examining in chapter four. In an early and powerful book, *Moral Man and Immoral Society*,[7] Niebuhr cites the case of the eighteenth century Bishop of London, writing to assure the slave-owners of the southern States that they need have no fear of Christian mission; for Christianity is concerned with freedom from the bondage of passion and desire and makes no difference to outward conditions and civil relations. It is not surprising that Marxists should take examples such as this to typify religion, still less that religion so understood should become the object of passionate moral criticism. But the examples do not have to be so extreme as that of the Bishop of London and the slaveowners. That example pinpoints in a highly exaggerated form the much more pervasive problem of the adequacy of Christian *social* ethics. Reinhold Niebuhr brings out very clearly the moral confusion caused by the exercise of individual responsibility and benevolence within a context of unjust social relationships. It is this more than anything else that has undermined Christian ethics in the nineteenth and twentieth centuries. Certainly the Marxist will denounce the gross moral outrages perpetrated by the Churches in the course of history – the Inquisition, the Crusades and the like – but, as we have already seen, the same list of abuses can be denounced by the self-critical Christian moralist. What is much more damaging is the accusation that Christian moral insight into the value of personal being and its encouragement of practical charity and self-sacrificial love – that is to say Christian ethics at their best – can mask and mollify the structural inequalities and injustices in the social order, and, as we have become increasingly aware, in the international economic order too. It is recognition of this combination of connivance in unethical and priveleged social and economic structures with the cultivation of practical love of the neighbour that induces moral confusion. For individual and personal benevolence, even at considerable cost to the giver, is bound to seem hypocritical if accompanied by blindness (wilful or unwilful) to unjust social relations.

Niebuhr also brings out how much worse this problem is

33

and is felt to be in modern urban and industrial society. For the individual and face-to-face relations of human benevolence are much more difficult to sustain in such conditions than in older feudal village communities. The unequal distribution of both power and wealth, reflected in the circumstances and attitudes of a man's class, cannot be obscured or made acceptable any longer by face-to-face personal attitudes and acts. We see some growing sensitivity to this in nineteenth century novels, such as Charlotte Bronte's *Shirley*, Mrs. Gaskell's *North and South* and many of Dickens' books. But 'a culture which tries to hide the cruelties by moral pretensions that do not change the facts makes cynics of those who know the facts', Niebuhr writes. The question then arises whether Christian ethics has the resources to confront this problem and meet it adequately – and indeed more adequately than the Marxist solution.

One way of meeting the problem is to point out that Jesus and the greatest of the Christian saints such as St. Francis explicitly recognised that pure love of the neighbour could only be shown by those who renounce the social and economic structures of the day. Only from outside the accepted social framework can the Christian bring the dimension of the love of God to bear on his fellow human beings in a pure way. But, quite apart from the question of whether this reflects a true assessment of the life and teaching of Jesus, it is a dangerous path for the defender of Christian ethics to tread. For it suggests that Christianity does not possess the resources for a valid social ethic; it concedes to the Marxist, say, the vision of a just social and economic order, in which the ideal of 'from each according to his ability to each according to his needs' is actually to be realised here on earth. As a matter of Christian history, as we all know, the Christian churches have never endorsed this step. They have attempted to draw from the Bible and the Christian tradition a social as well as an individual ethic. The dilemma for the student of the adequacy of Christian ethics is that again as a matter of Christian history by far the larger part of that social ethic has tended to sanctify rather than challenge the given social order. Today we see however a very different type of Christian social ethic being developed. Not that the Church has lacked those who, even in the nineteenth century, defended and expounded 'Christian socialism'; and much earlier glimpses of a Christian social ideal are to be found in the millenarian sects of the middle ages – unrealistic though they were at the time. But much more radical versions are common today in liberation theology and Christian Marxism, in which the gospel of the Kingdom of God is held to entail social revolution just as much as individual conversion.

But at this point we have to look at the other side of the coin, and raise the question of the moral ambiguities of Marxism, ambiguities which, many people claim, also characterise these fashionable Christian versions. I mentioned Reinhold Niebuhr's reference to the moral cynicism created in people's minds by the combination of individual charity and social privilege. And indeed moral cynicism, as Niebuhr goes on to show, is precisely what has characterised much Marxist thought and practice. If Christians have often shown a combination of high individual moral idealism with social blindness, Marxists have equally often shown a combination of egalitarian social idealism with individual moral cynicism. Christianity is certainly open to moral criticism for its tendency towards connivance in social injustice. But Marxism is certainly open to moral criticism for its much more overt and deliberate neglect of individual rights and values. Its willing-

ness to embrace any and every means to the achievement of
its egalitarian ends, its tendency to neglect the problems of
safeguards against the abuse of power by those who actually
hold the power in the name of the people, and indeed its very
subordination of individual ethics to social ethics (and sometimes its refusal to acknowledge even the moral nature of its
own social idealism) – all this is open to trenchant moral
criticism; and, in so far as Christian Marxism shares these
attitudes, it too is open to moral criticism and a questioning
of its pretensions to be a genuinely Christian stance.

There is an enormous literature on these issues and they
are central issues in the debate on the adequacy of Christian
ethics. Two books will be mentioned here, in order to illustrate the way in which the Marxist critique of Christianity is
being handled today. The first is *A Marxist looks at Jesus* by
Milan Machovec.[8] a book which illustrates both the possibilities and limitations of the Christian-Marxist dialogue that
took place in the sixties, particularly in Czechoslovakia in the
years prior to the ill-fated Dubcek experiment in 'socialism
with a human face' – that ideal itself being indicative of how
inhuman the communist countries were and are felt to be by
those who live in them. Machovec was Professor of Philosophy
in Prague from 1953–1970. The interest in and sympathy with
the figure of Jesus which he shows are an indication of a
greater openness and critical attitude on the part of Marxists.
The stereotyped Marxist attitude to religion as a matter of
alienation and fantasy is rejected here in favour of an attempt
to understand what was radical and new and genuinely human
in the life and teaching of Jesus. But the limitations of this
neo-Marxist approach are also evident. Machovec does not
permit himself to step outside the framework of atheistic
humanism and consider the possibility of a theistic grounding

36

of both individual and social ethics. The supposition that a critical humanism has the ability not only to sustain a profound moral vision but also to resist the abuses of power and interest is still an unquestioned assumption – a remarkable one in someone who had seen the Stalinist period from inside, and an assumption to be contrasted with the growing insight of Alexander Solzhenitsyn that the human spirit is not in the end of the day self-sustaining.

In the second place we may consider *The Contradiction of Christianity* by David Jenkins.[9] The importance of this book, which reflects the author's years as Director of Humanum Studies at the World Council of Churches in Geneva, lies in the way in which it brings out the contradictions both in historical Christianity and in Marxism, and the necessity of radical self-criticism enjoined by each upon the other. The inadequacy of much Christian faith and practice is shown up precisely by the entanglement of the Christian churches in dehumanising and oppressive structures. But equally the dehumanising effect of Marxism is shown up by its totalitarian tendencies and its neglect or denial of essential human values. This impasse leads Jenkins to ask if the Christian vision does not, after all, point to a transcendence in the midst of human contradictions, by which human relationships and human community might hope to be transfigured. He looks for both a radical politics and a radical spirituality, in which the resources of God are drawn on and relied on for the transformation of man and society. Jenkins offers no easy solution to the problem of the tension between acquiescence in oppression and acquiescence in the moral ambiguities of violent revolution. We shall return to this issue in chapter five.

This brief consideration of the legacy of the Marxist critique of religion has placed the second main question-mark against

37

the adequacy of Christian ethics, namely, its ability to sustain and realise an adequate social ethic. The first question-mark, which emerged from our reflections on Kant, Fichte and Hegel in chapter one, and which was highlighted again by the extreme figure of Nietzsche, concerned the inescapable heteronomy of Christian ethics. This second challenge concerns its inherent individualism. But whereas in the first case we shall be looking for a defence of heteronomy and attempting to show that ethics ultimately requires the notion of dependence on God, in the second case we shall have to deny the charge. This second challenge can be met only if can show that Christian ethics has, after all, the resources by which not only the individual but society may be transformed. The strength of the Marxist critique lies in the fact that, historically, Christianity has not actually succeeded in bringing about a just society. There is a sense in which Lenin achieved far more than any Christian and any Church have ever achieved. Yet Lenin's achievement was won at a cost which no Christian could sanction and has itself got caught in all too human ambiguity and contradiction. To defend the adequacy of Christian ethics in the social sphere would be to show that the potential for a lasting and humane social order requires the transcendent dimension and the larger hope of Christianity, and thus lies beyond the scope of any secular utopian theory or revolutionary practice.

We now turn to the criticism of religion by the founder of psychoanalysis, Sigmund Freud (1856–1939). Unlike Nietzsche and Marx, Freud was not concerned to advocate a 'transvaluation of values'. He claimed to be simply a scientist, offering an explanation for what he had long held to be an illusion.

Freud regarded religion as a product of wish fulfilment

38

'born from man's need to make his helplessness tolerable and built up from the material of memories of the helplessness of his own childhood and the childhood of the human race'.[10] We shall not follow him here into what he actually says about the childhood of the human race in his books *Totem and Taboo* and *Moses and Monotheism*, since, as an anthropological theory about the genesis of religion, it is wildly speculative and dismissed by anthropologists such as Evans-Pritchard as a just-so story for which there is no evidence whatever.[11] In fact, Freud's theory about the genesis of religion out of our own childhood experience (his 'ontogenetic' rather than his 'phylogenetic' theory) is much more interesting. The particular form which human wish-fulfilment takes in monotheistic religion, namely the idea of an omnipotent and righteous Father who provides the hostile universe with meaning, care and hope, is, for Freud, a projection on to the heavens of our childhood experience of dependence on adult protection. But not only do we replace our fallible human father, in this projection, by an all-powerful and infallible heavenly Father, we also transfer attitudes of guilt, and perpetuate infantile behaviour patterns in relation to this projected heavenly Father. Religion, then, is, for Freud, an illusion, hindering the scientific quest for truth and reality, and fixating an immature response to life. He calls it a 'universal obsessional neurosis' precisely because it leads to behaviour patterns dictated by repressed childhood feelings of guilt rather than by rational considerations.

A religious morality, therefore, is liable to be very inadequate indeed, since it presupposes not only an illusory dependence but also a neurotic one.

It is worth comparing Freud's views on religion with his views on morality in general. He does not think of morality as a neurotic phenomenon, though it can be that if, like religion, it perpetuates infantile attitudes. But a properly developed morality is, for Freud, a rational necessity, as indeed is civilisation itself. Freud held this view on utilitarian grounds. Man needs an individual and social morality. He does not need a religion. On the other hand Freud is equally ready to give a psychological account of the genesis of morality and civilisation. In his own terminology, the 'superego' internalises parental commands and makes them one's own, as the individual grows to maturity.

Such an account, for all Freud's perception of the rational necessity of morality for man in society, can have the unintended effect of undermining the authority of morals. The idea that conscience is the product of parental training in infancy, interiorised by the growing child, is far from the older idea of conscience as the voice of God. Moreover such an analysis can easily be adopted by the Marxists and made the basis for the rejection of 'bourgeois' conscience as proceeding from an upbringing in an unjust social class.

On the other hand, it is always possible to argue that psychological accounts of the genesis of moral ideas are one thing and questions of their truth, value and rationality are quite another. However deflating the popular effect of Freudian theory may have been, it has not prevented, and cannot in logic prevent, discussion amongst moral philosophers about the objectivity of morals. For it may be the case that values are real and objective over against us and yet have to be learned, appropriated and internalised in the manner Freud describes. A Freudian account of the genesis of moral concepts in the individual does not *have* to be regarded as an exhaustive account. It can, as it was for Freud himself, be allied with a utilitarian defence of man's need for morality. It *can* also be allied to a more objective theory of the good.

Can we construct a parallel argument where religious ideas are concerned? Admittedly, it does not follow from the psychological history of the acquisition of religious concepts in the individual or society that those concepts do not correspond with reality. It may be, as John Bowker has argued, that our projected ideas match up, to some degree, with reality over against us, and that the psychological mechanism of projection is simply the means whereby the human mind is furnished with ideas and concepts for, say, talking about God.[12] On any view, our actual conceptions of God are conditioned by our experience in childhood. But in order to defend religion and a religious ethic against Freud in this way, we would have to reject his extremely negative assessment of the basis of religious projections in wish-fulfilment and the neurotic repression of childhood guilt.

At this point we can turn the tables on Freud by questioning the narrow factual basis on which he erected his theories. Certainly a number of his patients in late nineteenth century Vienna showed neurotic and obsessional symptoms of a religious kind. But that does not justify universal generalisations about the nature of religion. On the contrary their inadequate and destructive character can equally well be diagnosed and treated in religious terms. Moreover Christian writers such as R. S. Lee, in his *Freud and Christianity*, and Harry Williams in his well-known essays and sermons, have used the insights of psychoanalysis to purify the theory and practice of Christianity from neurotic and repressive elements. On this view Freudian theory can be used to help the Christian to acquire self-awareness and a mature faith, including mature moral attitudes.

41

Psychoanalysis has a great deal to say about the liberation of men and women from neuroses, from behaviour patterns determined in infancy and beyond control because unconscious. Its aim is freedom from compulsions of this kind. But it has little to offer positively in terms of an ethical ideal. This is why its threat to the adequacy of Christian ethics is different from those of Nietzsche and Marx. Freud's own rational stoicism is *an* ethical ideal, but it must itself stand at the bar of criticism for its own truth and adequacy. Psychoanalysis constitutes a threat to a religious ethic only if the idea of a real religious object can be *demonstrated* to be both illusory and damaging, and if the neuroses in some religious people can be shown to be universal and inevitable consequences of religion as such. Needless to say, Freud never gets anywhere near establishing these theses.

It has become increasingly incumbent upon the apologist for a religious ethic not only to make these points against Freud but also to show that a religious ethic has the power to enhance and illuminate the life of man, and to provide what Freud does not provide, namely the ideal of and the resources for a perfected human life. We shall need to test the various versions of Christian ethics for their ability to do this.

It was suggested at the beginning of this chapter that the Anglo-Saxon mind would be more inclined to think of Darwin, Marx and Freud than Nietzsche, Marx and Freud as makers of the modern world. We may conclude the chapter with a few remarks about Charles Darwin (1809–1882).

We need not go into the controversies which followed the publication of *The Origin of Species* in 1859. It has long been recognised that the clash between evolutionary theory and the book of Genesis can be resolved by abandoning the literalist view of the latter. As one of Darwin's nieces observed: 'The

Bible says God made the world in six days, Uncle Charles says it took much longer; either way it's very wonderful'. On the other hand, the theory of evolution seemed to demolish what was left of the argument from design for the existence of God, and, sociologically speaking, it has predisposed subsequent generations to a naturalistic attitude. This has been well chronicled in Owen Chadwick's *The Secularisation of the European Mind in the Nineteenth Century.*[13] The development of Darwin's own religious opinions exemplifies this pattern. At the end of *The Origin of Species* he is still a theist. Life's powers had 'been breathed by the Creator into a few forms or into one.' He denied explicitly that he had meant to put forward atheistic views. Yet he became more and more agnostic towards the end of his life. He still felt something of the mystery of the beginning of all things, but the vast amount of suffering caused by evolution through natural selection struck him as a powerful argument against a benevolent God.

Darwin's ideas were seized on as the basis for a philosophy of life, including a moral philosophy, known as evolutionary ethics. But this was capable of application in widely different ways in social ethics, either in defence of laissez faire economics – the 'survival of the fittest' becoming the criterion of value – or in a Marxist sense– historical evolution, as understood in dialectical materialism. In moral philosophy today, evolutionary ethics is a dead duck. It was, of all theories, the one most easily demonstrated by G. E. Moore to have committed the naturalistic fallacy of simply *defining* 'good' as 'more evolved'.[14] In Christian thought, an evolutionary picture has been baptised in the thought of Teilhard de Chardin and in 'process' theology, but not, of course, as the basis for Christian ethics.

Consequently the chief challenge of Darwinism to the adequacy of Christian ethics is not that of an alternative ethic, like those of Nietzsche or Marx. It is more a negative challenge, like Freud's, to the plausibility and truth of a religious picture of the world. In particular it underlines the problem of evil, which any Christian ethic has got to make sense of before it can claim adequacy.

In this brief survey of major European writers since the Enlightenment, we have found a number of substantial criticisms of Christian ethics. Some have been part of wider attacks on the truth of the Christian religion, others more specifically addressed to its moral ideals, teaching and practice. We have seen its basis in the nature and will of God attacked as incurably heteronomous and destructive of human freedom and personality; we have seen its individualist bias attacked in favour of a man-centred social ethic; we have seen it attacked as fundamentally infantile and neurotic. Finally we have seen a question mark set against its plausibility in face of the evil and suffering entailed by the evolutionary process from which man has emerged. All the criticisms are supported by what can be presented as the dubious record of the churches in intolerance, fanaticism and so on. But the criticisms go much further than pointing to these facts. They are criticisms of principle. Consequently the defender of Christian ethics has to do more than point out that abuses such as the Inquisition represent aberrations of the Christian ideal. He has to show either that the more fundamental criticisms involve ideals which are themselves wrong in principle or that the Christian ideal has been misconceived by its critics, so that the criticisms do not really hit the mark. Finally, as we have stressed all along, he has to demonstrate the positive and creative moral power at the heart of the Christian tradition, making both for the individual and for the common good.

NOTES

1. A good selection of Nietzsche's writings is to be found in *The Portable Nietzsche*, ed. W. Kaufmann (London: Chatto and Windus, 1971). Also to be recommended are F. C. Copleston, *Friedrich Nietzsche: Philosopher of Culture* (London: Search Press 1942) and K. Jaspers, *Nietzsche and Christianity* (Chicago: Henry Regnery Co., 1961).
2. See W. Pannenberg, 'Types of Atheism and their Theological Significance' (as in note 5 to chapter one).
3. W. and L. Pelz, *God is No More* (London: Gollancz, 1963), and *True Deceivers* (London: Collins, 1966).
4. Harmondsworth: Penguin Books, 1971.
5. Martin Heidegger (1889–1976), the German existentialist philosopher, wrote a large two volume work on Nietzsche.
6. Harmondsworth: Penguin Books, 1975.
7. New York and London: Scribner's, 1936.
8. English trans., London: Darton, Longman and Todd, 1976.
9. London: SCM Press, 1976.
10. S. Freud, *The Future of an Illusion* (English trans., London: The Hogarth Press, 1928).
11. E. E. Evans-Pritchard, *Theories of Primitive Religion* (Oxford University Press, 1965), p. 42.
12. J. W. Bowker, *The Sense of God* (Oxford University Press, 1973), chapter six.
13. London: James Clarke, 1948.
13. Cambridge University Press, 1975.
15. G. E. Moore, *Principia Ethica* (Cambridge University Press 1903), chapter two.

CHAPTER THREE

Some Recent Critics of Christian Ethics

In this chapter, I extract a number of critical motifs from the writings of six twentieth century authors, who have been moved to attack Christianity and Christian ethics with greater or less ferocity. Not all contemporary moral philosophers feel it necessary to consider the Christian tradition, even critically. Secular ethics has long since gone its own way both analytically and constructively. But Christian ethics remains a target for a surprising number of writers, and it is instructive to see how the strands of criticism which we have noted from eighteenth and nineteenth century writers have been sharpened and developed more recently, and how certain further criticisms have been introduced.

The authors I have in mind are Bertrand Russell (1872–1970), one of the few great philosophers of the twentieth century, who, throughout his long life, combined a passionate ethical concern for social issues with an uncompromising hostility to religion;[1] Walter Kaufmann (b. 1921), for many years Professor of Philosophy at Princeton, whose name has already appeared in this book as an expositor of Hegel and Nietzsche;[2] Brand Blanshard (b. 1892), for many years Professor of Philosophy at Yale and a life-long apologist for the sole authority of reason;[3] Richard Robinson (b. 1902), who taught ancient philosophy and logic at Oriel College, Oxford;[4] Antony Flew (b. 1923), Professor of Philosophy at Reading University, who represents the tradition of Hume, and whose criticisms of the possibility and meaningfulness of religious language have been widely discussed in the philosophy of religion;[5] and Joachim Kahl (b. 1941), who was trained in theology as a Protestant pastor in Germany, reacted against the Church, left it, and proceeded to attack the Christian faith with the vehemence of a convert to Marxism.[6]

Let us now set out the criticisms which these authors make:
1. The first and most obvious line of criticism which they develop is condemnation of the past record of Christianity. Thus Russell sharpens Hume's negative assessment of Church history into a diatribe against Christianity's hostility to intelligence and science, its intolerance and its endorsement of primitive and childish attitudes. The greatest ages of faith, he declares, have involved the greatest cruelty, as in the Inquisition and the persecution of witches. He expatiates on how the Churches have retarded progress in social and sexual ethics. An even more hostile assessment of the balance sheet of Church history is given by Kahl. He lists the brutalities and inhumanities perpetrated by Christians – the treatment of slaves, pagans, Jews and heretics – and speaks of Christian defamation of sexuality and women. He argues that moral and social progress has come about through movements such as the Enlightenment, liberalism and Marxism, and specifically not through Christianity, which has fought a rearguard action against all these progressive movements.

The assessments are undoubtedly very selective and one-sided, though unfortunately there is much in Church history that can be selected to support such readings. There is much cause for shame and repentence in the history of the Churches.

Advocates of Christian ethics have no desire to defend these things. They will wish, no doubt, to paint the other side of the picture, and to insist that Christian ethics be ultimately judged by its highest ideals and potentialities. As was pointed out in chapter one, the abuses and aberrations to which critics point are condemned by Christians themselves when true to their ideals. But Kahl comes back with the more penetrating question. What does it mean that the religion which speaks of love has actually perpetrated these horrors in the course of history? For a religion which teaches 'by their fruits ye shall know them' this is a hard question indeed. One point is quite clear: if we are to insist on Christianity being judged at its best, in theory and in practice, we must extend this principle of charity to other religions and other moral systems as well. They too must be judged at their best – by their saints and by their ideals, as we should wish Christianity to be. The importance of this point will be stressed when we come to consider the ethical teachings of other religions in chapter six.
2. We have already seen how eighteenth and nineteenth century critics of Christian ethics press beyond enumeration of historical abuses to criticisms of principle. In a similar way our twentieth century critics proceed to suggest the even more damaging argument that religion is bound to have such deplorable effects as cruelty and intolerance. Russell argues that religious beliefs can only be passed on dogmatically by non-rational means. In such circumstances, harsh reaction against criticism and deviation is inevitable. Similarly Kaufmann holds that theology is unavoidably authoritarian and dogmatic, and Blanshard argues at length that belief which maintains itself and guides action irrespective of evidence and reason is itself immoral. In the sequel we shall need to probe our exponents of Christian ethics for their attitude to reason

and tolerance. It can hardly be denied that in the past the Christian Churches have often acted in the ways described by these authors. Whether this was really inevitable is a much more open question, as we shall see.

3. A further target for attack is the view that morality depends on religion. Flew, for example, reiterates the Euthyphro dilemma, which we discussed in chapter one.[7] arguing that a theistic basis for ethics can only make the good a matter of arbitrary divine will. He adds the point that often a religious ethic turns out to be a prudential ethic. The sacrifices it enjoins are strictly temporary, to be compensated by reward hereafter. Robinson points out the harmful effects of teaching the young that only religion can sustain morality. If people are taught to think of morality and religion as inseparable, when they lose religion, they lose morality as well. We note here the widely felt pedagogical importance of the autonomy of morals. Russell, as we have seen, believed that, far from fostering and sustaining moral attitudes and behaviour, religion has led to cruelty and intolerance.

One mark of adequacy in any version of Christian ethics to be considered in the chapters that follow is its ability to withstand this line of criticism. It has already been pointed out, in discussion of the Euthyphro dilemma, that the view that God is the ultimate source of all good need not prevent the moralist from holding that the good may be recognised independently in what makes for human flourishing. The relation between morality and religion is clearly more subtle than the crude relation of dependence which these critics have in mind.

There is an important point to be learned from this line of criticism. The Christian apologist must not overplay his hand. His argument can backfire, if he insists that the adequacy of

Christian ethics lies precisely in the absolute backing it gives to moral values through its doctrines of God and immortality. This becomes highly implausible if the consequence is drawn that a non-religious ethic has no meaning or value at all. Flew supposes that this is what is implied by Christian ethics and rejoins persuasively that values do not cease to be values because they are embodied or realised only fleetingly. This must be conceded. The point of Christian reference to absolute values lies not in a depreciation of the values already perceived but rather in their enhancement and greater illumination. To adapt a phrase of Aquinas', natural appreciation of the good is perfected, not destroyed, by recognition that it ultimately stems from God.

Robinson argues that harm is done to morality by the authoritarian connections of religious ethics. Again it has to be shown that the only proper authority possessed by Christian ethics is the authority of truth. Either it commends itself to the reason, heart and conscience of a man, or it is nothing.

4. A recurring theme in these philosophical critics of Christian ethics is their depreciation of faith as a virtue and their preference for reason and intelligence. Christianity has held that faith, hope and love constitute the 'theological virtues', the crown of the Christian ethical ideal. While tending to agree about the centrality of love, the critics question the other two. Robinson declares quite categorically that reason, joy and love are a better triad, Russell that the important virtues are kindness and intelligence. Elsewhere Russell states his belief that 'the good life is one inspired by love and guided by knowledge'. Blanshard criticises Jesus and the Christian tradition for their devaluation of reason. He holds that Christian ethics also tends to ignore certain other great goods of

human life, aesthetic values, for example, and those perhaps referred to in Robinson's preference for 'joy'.

The question of aesthetic values will be discussed in chapter seven. As far as joy is concerned, there is undoubtedly a problem about the tendencies towards extreme asceticism sometimes fostered in the Christian Church. A balanced view, however, will hardly deny the place of joy in the Christian scheme of things. But it is over the evaluation of intelligence, knowledge and reason that the dispute is likely to centre. Again it cannot be denied that there have been Christian writers, Tertullian and Kierkegaard among them, who have condemned man's reason and rejoiced in the irrationality of faith. This strand develops, one-sidedly, the powerful condemnation of the wisdom of this world in the letters of St. Paul. And there is indeed an arrogance and wilful blindness in some ways in which men exercise their rational powers. But mainstream Christianity has for the most part been quite ready to see in man's reason a divine gift and a reflection of the rationality of God, just as it has seen in human goodness a reflection of the goodness of God. However open to abuse men's recognition and exercise of these gifts may be, the love of truth and of every means of access to truth is as much a Christian virtue as it is a virtue for these philosophical critics. But, as we shall need to stress again and again, there are questions of truth at stake between the Christian and his critics. Writers such as Russell and Flew cannot be permitted to assume dogmatically that their understanding of reason and truth are beyond reproach and that commitment to science and common sense absolves them from attending to other less obvious sources of knowledge. It is quite unfair for Robinson to assert that religion buys its comforts at too high a price, 'namely at the price of abandoning the ideal of truth and

51

shackling and perverting man's reason'. Christianity claims to have learned that faith and hope are necessary to a full appreciation and realisation of man's nature and destiny. It follows that it is in the end irrational to depreciate these virtues. This means that reason and intelligence cannot be regarded as rivals to faith and hope. If faith and hope, at least for the course of our earthly pilgrimage, are given a place in Christian ethics second only to that of love, that is because those virtues are found to give access to ultimate truths, by which men can live as they were meant to live, and to which unaided reason and intelligence are blind. But it is arbitrary and irrational for reason to reject what lies beyond its own unaided powers. Moreover the Christian apologist will urge that, in the light of faith, the rationality of divine truth becomes apparent.

5. Further moral objections are levelled against certain Christian doctrines. In so far as Christian moral teaching is bound up with Christian doctrine – and this must be the case if Christianity is held to reveal the ultimate context of human action – then such objections are objections to Christian ethics too. Moral objections to Christian teaching about hell, for example, are common, not only from philosophers. Kaufmann singles out the doctrine of the Atonement for particular criticism. Many statements of these doctrines are indeed open to moral objection, and great harm is done to Christianity by attempts to defend the indefensible. But again we shall find our Christian moralists equally sensitive to these objections and we shall hope to find them capable of stating Christian doctrine in ways which enhance rather than flout men's moral sensibility.

The need to make sense of the problem of evil has already been mentioned. Both Flew and Blanshard regard this as the decisive objection to Christian belief in God. It is largely a moral objection. It is held to be morally intolerable that God should permit such evil and suffering in the world. To meet this objection a viable theodicy must be found. (The attempt to solve the problem of evil and to justify the ways of God with men is called 'theodicy'.) But it must itself be a morally credible theodicy. Unfortunately many theodicies that have been put forward, not only in the past, are themselves open to moral objection. Thus, if it is held that evil and suffering are permitted in order that virtues such as compassion and moral heroism shall be possible, it is rightly objected that this would often entail the use of someone else's suffering as a means to one's own or a third party's good. Christianity cannot commend itself by such morally outrageous arguments.[8]

6. Twentieth century writers feel much more free to criticise the ethical teaching of Jesus than did their predecessors, and it is fascinating to observe how these secular moralists react to the Sermon on the Mount. Russell allows the excellence of some of Christ's precepts, such as 'Resist not evil', 'Judge not lest ye be judged', 'Give to him that asketh' – though he notes that few Christians live up to those maxims. But he criticises Christ's teaching about hell, his ferocity in denouncing the scribes and Pharisees, his belief in the imminence of the end of the world, and his cursing of the fig tree. Kaufmann is particularly critical of the reward motif in the Sermon on the Mount. He contrasts this prudential element in the Gospels – one is to lose one's life *in order to* gain it – with the utterly disinterested morality of the Buddhist teacher who said that if there is a hell, he would wish to forgo heaven for himself in order to share the sufferings of those in hell. Robinson, like Russell, notes a strain of harshness in the ethical teaching of Jesus, and, like Kaufmann, condemns the element of re-

ward and threat. He detects five main strands in Jesus' teaching: the commands to love God, to have faith in Jesus himself, to love one's neighbour including one's enemies, to achieve purity of heart or motive, and to exercise humility. Robinson rejects the first two injunctions, holding their justification to be unclear and their tendency to sanction the overriding of ordinary moral claims; he accepts the third – to love the neighbour – though he questions universal non-resistence (as does Blanshard in his treatment of this theme); he questions the fourth precept, purity of motive, on the grounds that it involves a narrowing of the imagination; and on the fifth he observes that truth and respect are more important than humility. Both Robinson and Blanshard hold that, in any case, the teaching of Jesus is one-sided (though Blanshard is more appreciative of the positive quality of Jesus' love ethic). The Sermon on the Mount, they observe, contains little or nothing on beauty, knowledge or reason; its valuation of poverty is excessive; and it can hardly form the basis of a social ethic.

It is very interesting to read these assessments of the ethical teaching of Jesus by secular moralists. There are, of course, many points on which they disagree amongst themselves (as over the value of humility) and some judgements which even at first reading carry little conviction (such as Robinson's comments on purity of motive). Moreover the interpretations of what Jesus actually meant are often controversial. To take an example to which we shall be returning, it seems quite clear that whatever else the ethical teaching of Jesus was it was not prudential. Christian moralists understand love of God and love of the neighbour as the only proper response to absolute good and unqualified need respectively. We shall see in the next chapter how New Testament scholars such as Joachim Jeremias and moral theologians such as Kenneth

Kirk interpret the alleged 'reward' motif in the Sermon on the Mount. To take another example, it simply is not true to say, with Blanshard, that Jesus glorified extreme poverty. A balanced judgement will weigh up all Jesus' dealings with the rich and with the poor, and will look for the point of his stressing the spiritual dangers in addiction to material goods and wealth. Again we might contrast Blanshard's objections to the implications of some of the parables of Jesus (such as the Labourers in the Vineyard – Blanshard thinks that it implies approval of arbitrary actions by property-owners!) with Iris Murdoch's judgement: 'Certain parables . . . undoubtedly owe their power to the fact that they incarnate a moral truth which is paradoxical, infinitely suggestive and open to continual reinterpretation'.[9] She has seen the point of the parables of Jesus, while Blanshard has not. Blanshard cavils at totally irrelevant generalisations from details of the stories.[10]

One major problem in assessing these secular responses to the recorded teaching of Jesus stems from their insistence on seeing the core of Christian ethics in a straightforward acceptance of the precepts of Jesus just as they stand. Kaufmann, for example, refuses to take the Christian ethics of Reinhold Niebuhr seriously, on the grounds that Niebuhr's interpretation strays too far from the explicit teaching of the New Testament. Similarly Robinson and Blanshard neglect the difference of context between New Testament and modern times, and ignore the possibility that principles may be discerned in and extracted from the words of Jesus that can be made the basis of Christian judgement on problems and situations quite unknown in the world of the New Testament. Above all, these critics of the teaching of Jesus, in scrutinising his precepts simply as they stand, fail to reckon with their purpose of opening up a living relation to the God who is revealed not simply in the words, but in the whole life and passion of Jesus – a relation which, as we shall see, becomes the living source of Christian thought and action in each generation of believers.

7. We may conclude this list of the different strands in twentieth century criticism of Christian ethics by noting the recurrent condemnation of its individualism. The point is made against both the teaching of Jesus and against Christian ethics generally. Russell declares that Christianity's emphasis on the soul has made its ethics completely individualistic. Kaufmann, interestingly, expresses preference for the social ethic of the Old Testament over the teaching of Jesus about individual salvation, thus ignoring the fact that Jesus in no way repudiated the former, and that the Old Testament continues to be an important source for Christian ethics too. But the most virulent critic on this score is once again Kahl, who repeats the Marxist criticism of the Christian moral tradition along the lines sketched in the last chapter. We have already undertaken to examine modern Christian ethics for its ability to meet this line of criticism.

Two points may be made here as we look back over these seven strands in twentieth century criticism, and before we turn to examine a number of significant presentations of a Christian ethic for today. The first has already been raised in discussion of these critics' passion for reason and truth. We shall, of course, agree that where it can be shown that truth is being concealed or the search for truth impeded, there must be moral protest from Christian and non-Christian alike. But the question of truth must not be begged. It is to be noted that many of the moral objections to Christian ethics which we have surveyed depend on the prior rejection of Christianity as false and on the consequent assumption that advocacy of a specifically Christian morality is irrational. But no one can dogmatically assume a monopoly of truth. To read Russell's famous radio debate with Copleston is to realise how in the moral sphere unsolved questions of truth and falsity are at stake. Can the difference between right and wrong be ultimately grounded in the being and nature of God? Does the moral consciousness of man reflect an incipient awareness of that absolute source of all good, or is it, as Russell says, easily explained in terms of childhood instruction by nurses and parents. Can an account of human moral sensitivity be given purely in terms of human feeling, as Russell thinks? These are serious questions and neither side in these disputes should be permitted to assume that these issues have been resolved. Each position deserves to be explored and tested for its theoretical as well as for its practical adequacy.

In the second place, mention of practical adequacy raise the question of the resources available to any system of ethics for the transformation of lives and society. We have to ask whether the kindness and love advocated by Russell, or the humility, love, courage and honesty advocated by Kaufmann, or the reason, joy and love advocated by Robinson, are actually within the power of unaided human nature to achieve. Certainly some people are benevolent. Hume and the British moralists were right to stress the fact of human sympathy as one of the springs of moral feeling and practice. But are not Russell, Kaufmann and Robinson reduced simply to recommending the virtues which they list, with no actual resources for doing something about human wickedness and human inability to live up to man's best ideals? They can of course appeal to the influence of education; Russell, indeed, with admirable consistency, founded and ran a progressive school.

Other more militant secular moralists believe that human nature can be changed and social conditions transformed by violent revolution. Transformation of conditions can certainly be achieved that way. But there is a great deal of evidence now to suggest that human nature is not changed by such violent structural change and that man's inhumanity to man reappears in even worse forms of the abuse of power. Something has been said about this problem already and more will be said in chapter five. But if the resources available to secular moralists for the transformation of man are so negligible or so crude, ought we not to look again at the religious resources claimed by Christians and others to be offered to man for his redemption or salvation? Like the secular moralists, Christians recommend kindness, love, humility, courage and honesty. But these are not just ideals. Christianity has been found to contain spiritual resources to change men's lives, not just to reinforce a benevolence already there. Men have received the inspiration and the power to do things which they did not have it in themselves to do. To stress this point is to refer again to the fact that Christian moral life is believed to rest on and to flow from a living spiritual relation. The virtues mentioned here are believed to be fruits of the Spirit. Once again it seems that we are speaking of individual transformation; but the question of alternative resources for social transformation to those of violent revolution remains on the agenda for this book. The exponents of Christian ethics whom we study in the next two chapters have not neglected this problem.

As we turn now to examine a number of versions of Christian ethics, we shall need to test them for their ability to meet the recurring criticisms which we have encountered – the problems, that is, of truth, honesty, tolerance and freedom, the questions of autonomy, maturity and scope. We shall need to scrutinise them for their social adequacy and press the question whether their social conservatism or radicalism is a matter of embracing alien secular pressures, in the manner castigated by the 1978 Reith Lecturer,[11] or whether it is rather a matter of eliciting something fundamentally and in principle Christian.

Whatever we discover on these issues and whatever creative and illuminating insights we may find over and above the ability of Christian ethics to withstand criticism, it has to be admitted that the past contains many horrors perpetrated in the name of the Christian religion. Of all the points made against Christianity, this question of Kahl's remains the most challenging: What does it mean that the religion which speaks of love – and, we may now add, the religion which claims the divine gift of love – has actually perpetrated these things in the course of history? Something will have to be said about that persistent incubus upon the plausibility of Christianity as a vehicle of the good.

NOTES

1. B. Russell, *Why I am not a Christian* (London: Allen and Unwin, 1957).
2. W. Kaufmann, *Critique of Religion and Philosophy* (New York: Harper and Row, 1958) and *The Faith of a Heretic* (New York: Doubleday, 1961).
3. B. Blanshard, *Reason and Belief* (London: Allen and Unwin, 1974).
4. R. Robinson, *An Atheist's Values* (Oxford University Press, 1964).
5. A. Flew, *God and Philosophy* (London: Hutchinson, 1966) and *The Presumption of Atheism* (London: Elek/Pemberton, 1976).
6. J. Kahl, *The Misery of Christianity* (English trans., Harmondsworth: Penguin Books, 1971).
7. See pp. 13f. above.

8. On the problem of evil, see B. Hebblethwaite, *Evil, Suffering and Religion* (London: Sheldon Press 1976).

9. I. Murdoch, 'Vision and Choice in Morality', in *Proceedings of the Aristotelian Society* 1956, and reprinted in I. T. Ramsey (ed.), *Christian Ethics and Contemporary Philosophy* (London: SCM Press, 1966).

10. For further discussion of moral objections to the teaching of Jesus, see Errol E. Harris, *Atheism and Theism*, Tulane Studies in Philosophy, Vol XXVI (New Orleans 1977), chapter VII, and R. H. Preston, 'Ethical Criticisms of Jesus' in A. Hanson (ed.), *Vindications* (London: 1966).

11. E. R. Norman, *Christianity and the World Order* (Oxford University Press, 1979).

CHAPTER FOUR

Christian Ethics in the Light of Criticism

How, in the light of the criticisms which we have been examining can Christian ethics profess to provide even an adequate, still less a final and definitive account of the right and the good for man in both his individual and his collective life? One point needs to be made at the onset. No one presentation of Christian ethics will itself be final or even adequate. As with all other branches of theology and indeed of philosophy, any one man's view or any specific school or tradition is bound to suffer from the limitations, distortions and approximations which characterise human thought about anything. When we speak of the adequacy of Christian ethics, we are not speaking only of particular formulations or presentations, but rather of that which men and women in the Christian tradition claim to have perceived or learned, however inadequately, about the right and the good. This is why the Christian moralist can often agree with or at least see the point of criticisms made by secular moralists. Not surprisingly the critic tends to fasten on the least adequate aspects of any one presentation. The apologist seeks to shift attention to the ideal behind the imperfect presentation. Critic and apologist meet in straight conflict only when a genuine clash between different ideals is in question.

With this caveat in mind, we turn to a number of twentieth century presentations of Christian ethics, in order to test them for their adequacy, and in particular, for their ability to withstand the criticisms which have preoccupied us so far.

The first Christian moralist to be considered is Kenneth Kirk (1886–1954). Kirk was one of the leading Anglican moral theologians of the twentieth century. Before becoming Bishop of Oxford in 1937, he was Regius Professor of Moral and Pastoral Theology in the University of Oxford. His best known book is *The Vision of God*, on which we shall be concentrating; but *Some Principles of Moral Theology* and *Conscience and Its Problems* should also be consulted.[1]

A highly impressive feature of Kirk's writings is his command of the enormous amount of material, both on the principles of Christian ethics and on the detailed applications of moral theology and casuistry that has been built up in the Roman Catholic Church on the basis of the teaching of St. Thomas Aquinas and in the Anglican Church by the Caroline divines such as Jeremy Taylor. ('Casuistry', as its name implies, means the application of law and conscience to particular cases and circumstances.) We are primarily concerned in this book with basic principles, but it is important to realise that the Christian tradition also contains a vast accumulation of detailed applications on the basis of pastoral experience. Kirk, in fact, makes a sharp distinction between Christian ethics and moral theology, the former being concerned with basic principles and ultimate ideals, the latter being concerned with minimum Christian standards, with what is permissible, and with the limits beyond which no one, and certainly no Christian, ought to step. This kind of distinction and the detailed casuistry that goes with concentration on moral theology in Kirk's sense, have fallen into disrepute in more recent writing on Christian ethics, which, as we shall see in the next chapter, has shared the tendency of secular ethics to concentrate on general principles and ideals, and to leave the detailed decisions for people to make themselves according to their own conscience. In other words, recent Christian ethics too has tended to rebel at least against Church or priestly authority in matters of moral decision. But Kirk's work reminds us of the fund of practical experience available to help people make their moral decisions, and we shall see reason to question the recent tendency to suggest that every moral decision should be made by reference to very general principles such as those of truth and love. It is far from clear that this is an adequate suggestion in the face of the concrete complexities of actual moral choice.

Nevertheless our own concern is, at present, with the more general questions of principle, and so attention must be focused on Kirk's treatment of the Christian ideal, the 'summum bonum', which he sees in terms of the title of his Bampton Lectures, as the vision of God. Despite his awareness of the need for moral rules and detailed casuistry, Kirk sees the aim of Chritian ethics as growth into personal union with Christ, such as to leave the need for rules behind. The character of disinterested love is, as it were, simply to flow from this mystical vision. This conception is basically Augustinian. The vision of God and union with God in Christ are man's true end and the virtues are the natural accompaniment and outcome of progressive realisation of that end.

Particular interest attaches to the way in which Kirk deals with the reward motif in the Gospels.[2] This, we saw, looms large in the criticisms of the teaching of Jesus by Kaufmann and Robinson. But, for Kirk, disinterested love is of the essence of the teaching of Jesus. He devotes many pages to showing that the main tendency in Jesus' teaching is towards helping men 'to forget themselves by focussing all their aspirations upon God and the kingdom of God, and upon the needs of men as seen with the eyes of God'. Consequently the apparent prominence of the reward motif in many parables and sayings of Jesus constitutes a considerable difficulty for Kirk. He meets it by the suggestion that the reward motif in the teaching of Jesus was not meant as an inducement to disinterestedness and self-sacrifice. That would be self-contradictory. You cannot have prudential motive for disinterestedness. But neither should disinterestedness be cultivated for its own sake. A truly disinterested act is one inspired by love of God and the neighbour. So Jesus' reference to the ultimate context and consequence of human action is part of his method of getting people to think about God and His goodness. Men are not to make reward their goal, but neither are they to cultivate self-sacrifice for its own sake. 'Leaving behind thoughts both of reward and disinterestedness as equally self-centred, they are to look forward to that true self-forgetfulness which cannot be acquired by human effort, but comes only to those whose hearts are set on God.'

I notice a similar treatment of the reward motif in the work of the New Testament scholar, Joachim Jeremias.[3] He suggests that the proper motive for Christian response to Jesus and his teaching is gratitude for the divine love, and that the talk of reward is simply a spelling out of that divine love in terms of the consequences of the removal of barriers between man and God.

This kind of interpretation, stressing ultimate consequence and context as a way of opening men's eyes to the nature and activity of the divine source of all good, is perhaps born out by the fact that reward is not in fact apportioned in accordance with merit in the parables of Jesus. The owner of the vineyard gives the same wage to those who worked only from the eleventh hour as he does to those who bore the heat and burden of the say. This parable, which gave such puritanical offence to Blanshard, has to be understood as a parable of the divine grace.

To return to Kirk's conception of the vision of God, it is clear that an ethic which is seen to flow from growth into mystical union is very different from a secular ethic which can only recommend certain ideal virtues or hope to evoke sympathy and care by pointing to human need. Its claim to greater adequacy is a function of its claim to recognise in God the source of all men's good and the resources for overcoming alienation and sin and for transforming lives.

We have seen how such an ethic meets the charge of prudential motives. How might it be thought to meet the other main charges of heteronomy and individualism?

On the question of heteronomy, the apologist for a Christian ethic such as Kirk's can only reply that the notions of autonomy and heteronomy are incurably ambiguous. Certainly the detailed casuistry is in danger of overriding human moral freedom; but the ideal of the vision of God takes us on to a plane where it becomes absurd to assert man's independence against the very source of his own good. Man finds his true freedom in relation to the source of all being and value. There is no arbitrary heteronomy here, nor is man's moral autonomy overridden. In embracing the love that made him, a man's own nature as a lover of God and his fellow men begins to be realised. Of course there is plenty of room for error in the appropriation of this fundamental Christian insight.[4]

The objection of excessive individualism is a much more powerful objection to an interpretation of Christian ethics such as Kirk's. It is true that Kirk is quite well aware that the notion of the vision of God is not the only way of expressing the Christian conception of the summum bonum. It is also powerfully symbolised by such notions as 'the Kingdom of God'. Moreover there is interesting discussion in Kirk's book of Augustine on the 'City of God'. Here Kirk tries to bring out the more positive side of Augustine's teaching about the earthly city as well as about the heavenly city. Nor does Kirk neglect the social dimension of the ethic of disinterested love, which, he holds, flows from growth into the knowledge of God in Christ. But it is undeniable that both in its minimal (casuistic) and maximal (vision of God) senses Kirk's moral ideal is primarily one of individual conscience and individual perfection and union with God. In a sense, this must be so, for it is individuals who have to act; but one is bound to admit that Christian social ethics get insufficient treatment in Kirk's writings.

To read Kirk after reading the critics of Christianity is to be driven back to the question of resources for the realisation of ideals. Secular moralists undoubtedly show and teach a strong sense of justice, honesty and benevolence; but Christians speak of a divine-human relation out of whose resources men and society are to be transformed. The question at issue is a question of truth. Are men alone in the universe and able only to inspire and encourage each other with ideals of life, or are there resources beyond their own that make for the transformation and eventual perfection of human beings and human community?

The second exponent of Christian ethics to be considered is Karl Barth (1886–1968). Barth incorporates his treatment of ethics in his monumental, unfinished work, *Church Dogmatics*. His is in every sense a theological ethic. For Barth

66

there can be no dogmatics without ethics and no ethics without a theological basis. It is only from within our knowledge of God's revelation of himself in Jesus Christ as our creator, reconciler and redeemer that proper ethical action and reflection can take place. The whole *Church Dogmatics* reflects this basic assumption. Each major section ends (or would have ended) with an extended treatment of the ethical implications of what has gone before. The first two part-volumes, containing the Prolegomena, the 'Doctrine of the Word of God', conclude with a section entitled 'Dogmatics as Ethics', in which Barth underlines the necessity of ethics for dogmatics. To quote from this section: 'A reality which is conceived and presented in such a way that it does not affect or claim men or awaken them to responsibility or redeem them, i.e., a theoretical reality, cannot possibly be the reality of the Word of God, no matter how great may be the richness of its content or the profundity of its conception.'

The next two part-volumes, containing the 'Doctrine of God', end with a chapter on 'The Command of God', in which Barth reverses the usual sequence of Law and Gospel, and presents the command of God as following from the Gospel as grace in action. So far, Barth's treatment is pretty general and formal; but his intention was to deal with special ethics and concrete problems at the end of each of the remaining major divisions of the Church Dogmatics, on creation, reconciliation and redemption. We have the 'Creation' volumes complete, and the whole of the last of the four part-volumes is devoted to 'The Command of God the Creator', beginning with a long section on man's freedom before God. Barth goes on to deal with marriage, the family, the neighbour, respect for life, and such topics. Remembering that Barth refuses to treat creation apart from Christology, it should not surprise us to find all this determined by what God has done for man in Christ.

The 'Reconciliation' volumes were never completed. *Church Dogmatics* ended with a fragmentary volume on baptism from the ethics section. But Barth was lecturing on 'The Command of God the Reconciler' in the academic years 1959–61 and this was the material that would have been worked up into the last of the 'Reconciliation' volumes. These lectures have been published in German in the edition of Barth's complete works which is being issued from Zurich. They contain a lengthy exposition of the opening clauses of the Lord's Prayer. The final chapter is entitled 'The Battle for Human Justice' and contains fascinating material on political ethics.

The 'Redemption' volumes were never even begun, though they would have ended with a chapter on 'The Command of God the Redeemer', thus completing the trinitarian pattern of Barth's theological ethics.[5]

Whatever else we may find ourselves wanting to say about Barth's ethics, we shall not find him wanting in the area where we were most unsure of Kirk's adequacy as an exponent of Christian ethics. Barth's commitment to political action is well known. In his early period as a pastor he was a thoroughgoing socialist. At that time he even went so far as to say that 'socialism is a predicate of the Gospel'. His leadership in the early days of the German Confessing Church's struggle against Hitler – before he was expelled to his native Switzerland – is also well known, as is his refusal to adopt an uncritical anti-communism in the post-war period. There has in fact been a lively debate in Germany, in recent years, over the degree of Barth's political radicalism,[6] a debate which cannot be examined here; but there can be no doubt that this aspect of Barth's ethics gives the lie to Reinhold Niebuhr's view that 'Barth's theology is too transcendent to offer any guidance for the discriminating choices that political responsibility challenges us to.'[7] It was indeed Barth's concern that Christians and the Church should listen for and follow the will of God in all areas of life and most specifically in social and political life. The prayer 'Thy Kingdom come' commits the man who prays it to the struggle for human justice. But it is also true that, for Barth, theological ethics, with its transcendent standpoint, would not permit us to identify any human achievement or programme with the Kingdom. For this reason, he would no longer say categorically that socialism is entailed by the Gospel.

Readers of Barth's ethical writings will quickly become aware of the problem of what precisely Barth means by the command of God. This is comparable to the problem of what precisely he means by the word of God today. In each case, Barth's 'actualism', as it has been called, prevents us from pinning down specific injunctions. The command of God, like the word of God, is each time an actual event in the here and now, *in* the given context and *to* men and women in that context. Just as Barth proceeds in the faith that the theologian, like any Christian man, will hear the living word of God in and through the Church's proclamation, so he proceeds in the faith that the man who remains true to God's gift of himself in the revelatory and reconciling work of Jesus Christ will hear the command of God for every situation in which he finds himself. In face of this command, man must simply obey. This is the law which follows from the Gospel. It is the way the Gospel claims a man in his own life-situation. Certainly the theologian, reflecting on the revelatory and reconciling work of Jesus Christ will be able to discern the general shape of human life lived in obedience to God's will. This is the form taken by Barth's own ethical writings. But each Christian man, in his actual situation, has to hear the specific command of God for himself and act upon it without any further deliberation. Such is Barth's extraordinary confidence in the actual operation of the living God in and upon the believer. Not on the believer in isolation, of course; for the believer must act as a member of a body, the Church of Christ, as, for example, Barth himself acted in leading the Confessing Church's struggle against Hitler at the time of the Barmen Declaration in 1934.

This theological actualism, which makes the notion of God's specific command a highly elusive notion to discuss, should not be understood as overriding man's freedom. On the contrary, to quote Barth, 'all man's activity is freedom for God and responsibility before Him'. God's claim on man is met by man's freedom for God. Here, it seems, Barth and Kirk would agree. Man finds his true freedom in obedient response to God.

This very powerful theological ethic, which needs to be read at length if one is to do any justice to it at all, faces one outstanding difficulty, which must be glaringly obvious in the light of our previous reflections in this book. It gives no room, it seems, for non-theological ethics, or for the recognition of natural human goodness outside the covenant of grace. One can understand why even those who admire Barth's stand against Hitler wish that he could have spoken simply in the name of humanity rather than exclusively in terms of the Lordship of Christ. It is true that, in rejecting the idea of an independent philosophical ethic, Barth is not denying that there is such a thing as human goodness and conscience, and indeed he praises Kant for his formulation of the categorical imperative;[8] but, for Barth, all this is in itself ultimately unintelligible until annexed by divine self-revelation. It is theological ethics that renders the claim under which man stands intelligible by showing that it stems from the grace of God in Jesus Christ.

The implication of this theological stance is that criticism from outside can never be in a position to establish itself against Christian ethics. Nevertheless it is part of the fascination of Barth that, despite his theological extremism, the *Church Dogmatics* contains a wealth of illuminating comment on authors such as Kant, Feuerbach, Marx and Nietzsche. This can well be illustrated by referring to Barth's treatment of Nietzsche. The topic of Nietzsche is raised in the course of Barth's exposition of the Christian doctrine of man.[9] True to his Christocentric method, Barth begins with Jesus Christ as the man for other men, and proceeds, on that basis, to treat the basic form of humanity as 'fellow-humanity'. Christian anthropology, says Barth, has to reject, from the very start, any purely individualist ideal. Consequently, we go astray at once if we base our understanding of man on the assertion, 'I am'. This is where Barth's treatment of Nietzsche comes in; for Nietzsche sought to develop a conception of Olympian self-sufficiency. He wanted to set himself up, like Zarathustra, 'six thousand feet beyond man and time and soar like an eagle, way above humanity'. The necessity for Nietzsche's fierce polemic against Christ and Christianity, says Barth, stemmed precisely from his perception, in the crucified man for others, of an exactly opposite ideal. Barth concludes his analysis of Nietzsche's position by praising him for bringing out, by this sharp contrast, what Christianity's essence is – its insistence that man is made to be man for others and that our common humanity is to be discovered in the weak and poor and suffering.

71

Clearly this theological ethic is set to meet all challenges head on. Barth believed that uncompromising faithfulness to the God of the Christian Gospel alone provided the proper perspective for identifying, proclaiming and fulfilling the good for man and society.

Our problem with this approach is partly the difficulty, if not impossibility, of achieving or sustaining such a pure standpoint. Barth's theology, after all, is a human construction like any other, and it contains its own imbalances and distortions. For instance, it is far from clear that Barth does justice to human freedom in its powers of responsible deliberation about what is to be done in a given situation. Nor is it clear that command and obedience are really the best model for articulating the dependence of man on the God who is the source and goal of all his good. But the chief problem is that a Barthian approach fails to do justice to ordinary and extraordinary human goodness, as they manifest themselves outside the sphere of Christian revelation and response, and which, as we have seen, can become the basis of independent moral criticism of empirical Christianity. While it is quite reasonable to set out the structure of a theological anthropology and ethics, both individual and social, in terms of the nature and will of God, it must be possible also to operate with a doctrine of creation that makes sense of human goodness outside the explicit Christian faith.

The next exponent of Christian ethics to be considered is Dietrich Bonhoeffer (1906–1945), particularly in his unfinished and posthumously published book, *Ethics*.[10] Readers of Bonhoeffer's treatment of the Sermon on the Mount, in his earlier book, *The Cost of Discipleship*, will be aware of two major difficulties. In the first place, despite his admirable insistence on the concreteness of the command of God as it came to men through the lips of Jesus, there was a certain literalness in Bonhoeffer's approach to the Sermon on the Mount which seemed to ignore the complexities of moral problems in the very different context and situation of today – a literalness curiously comparable to that of critics of the Sermon such as Kaufmann. And secondly, as with Barth, there seemed to be no serious reckoning with the facts of human goodness outside the sphere of divine grace and man's response to it. In fact, unlike Barth, Bonhoeffer did allow certain Lutheran qualifications to modify this position. For instance, in his section on 'Revenge', he rightly stressed the renunciation of resistance and revenge as an explicit command of Jesus, but then added: 'If we took the precept of non-resistance as an ethical blueprint for general application, we should indeed be indulging in idealistic dreams; we should be dreaming of a utopia with laws which the world would never obey. To make non-resistance a principle for secular life is to deny God by undermining his gracious ordinance for the preservation of the world.' The implication of this strong language is that there are two distinct forms of the divine will for man, general ordinances for secular man, and special injunctions for Christian disciples, who are called to tread the way of the Cross. This may be so, but the problems of such a disjunction for a viable Christian ethical theory are very great. Moreover it is precisely this kind of disjunction that Bonhoeffer seeks to overcome in his later book, *Ethics*.

Despite its unfinished state, *Ethics* contains some extremely pertinent material, illustrating both Bonhoeffer's longstanding insistence on the concreteness of the divine claim on a man, and his newer search for unity and reconciliation as the Christian task in the world. No longer is the world seen as an alien sphere, subject only to divine ordinances which keep it from

73

utter chaos; rather it is now seen as precisely the sphere in which God is active and which God is seeking to conform to his will. The world as such is now claimed for Christ, in all its 'mundane' reality, including its ethics. The world is the sphere of Christian responsibility, both individually and socially.

Bonhoeffer's *Ethics* is still very much a Christian theological ethic. It takes its starting point from the way in which God overcomes the split between the ideal and the real in Jesus Christ. Jesus Christ is reality as it was meant to be. Consequently conformity to Jesus Christ is conformity to reality, and the task of ethics is seen as that of finding Christ in the world and bringing the world more and more into conformity with him. The way in which this is to be done is worked out much more carefully and with much greater sensitivity to the actual complexities of life than in the earlier exposition of the Sermon on the Mount. In particular Bonhoeffer now shows an awareness of the implicit presence of Christ in the world already in the natural concerns and relationships of people, in what Bonhoeffer calls 'the structures of responsible life'.

This crucial recognition that God in Christ is there already in the world of human concerns makes possible a much more balanced conception of the relation between theological and secular ethics than we found in Barth's writings. Bonhoeffer expresses this insight in terms of 'ultimate' and 'penultimate' claims. The ultimate claim of the Gospel of redemption sends man back into the world to find God there in the midst of the penultimate claims of nature and culture.

This is a remarkable development for a Lutheran theologian, himself caught up in one of the greatest perversions of natural man – the Nazi tyranny – that the world has ever known. The story of his involvement in the 1944 plot against

Hitler and his execution at the hands of the Nazis shortly before the end of the Second World War is well known.

Bonhoeffer's position can perhaps best be illustrated by his treatment of the doctrine of the Fall of man; for it is that doctrine which makes Protestant theology of the Barthian type so suspicious of any attempt to build bridges between the Christian ethic of redemption and any secular ethic. Bonhoeffer is not willing to equate the natural with the fallen state of man. Granted that natural man does not exist in the direct state of dependence on God for which he was created, there still remains the difference between the natural and the unnatural, between the true and the wrong use of the freedom of man's natural life. In the sphere of man's 'penultimate' concerns, there is, as Bonhoeffer puts it, 'relative openness' and 'relative closedness' for Christ. This is still a Christocentric position; but the crucial difference from Barth lies in the fact that Bonhoeffer is able to take seriously the sphere of the penultimate – man's natural freedom and responsibility – as already relatively open to the presence and activity of God in Christ. This is what makes it possible (and necessary) for the Christian to *look for* Christ in the world, not just to bring Him to it.

Something will be said at the end of this chapter on the degree of success with which all these versions of Christian ethics might be thought to meet the criticisms and accusations of inadequacy which were listed in the previous chapters. But there is one feature of Bonhoeffer's position which particularly stands out and calls for immediate comment. That is his insistence on the way in which Christ closes the gap between the ideal and the real. We observed earlier that secular moralists such as Russell, Kaufmann and Robinson seemed to be reduced simply to bewailing men's actual attitudes and rec-

ommending certain virtues as ideal. Christian ethics, by contrast, according to Bonhoeffer, with its insistence on
redemption and renewal through Christ at least offers a means
of closing this gap between the ideal and the real in conformity
with the One in whom that gap was fully overcome. Admittedly there may well still be disputes about the nature of the
ideal, disputes, that is, about the proper interpretation of the
mind of Christ. But the strength of Christianity must surely
lie in its recognition both of the realisation of the ideal in the
person of Jesus and the possibility of its realisation, however
approximately, in those who are being conformed to him.

The last exponent of Christian ethics, selected for examination in this chapter, is Reinhold Niebuhr (1892–1971) a
writer already mentioned in this book as being particularly
sensitive to the weakness of Christian social ethics in the past.
We shall indeed find Niebuhr to be the most profound and
creative exponent of Christian social ethics, although it may
be thought that he achieved his insight into the relation between the absolute love ethic of Jesus and the complexities
and compromises of human social life at the cost of some
neglect of the elements which we have found stressed in Kirk,
Barth and Bonhoeffer, namely, the relation of the individual
to the living Christ. It is interesting that when Bonhoeffer
visited Union Theological Seminary in New York in 1939 he
singled Niebuhr out in his report on American Christianity as
the most significant and creative of American theologians,
but, while praising his critical stance on social ethics, he noted
the omission from Niebuhr's work of a doctrine of the redemptive work of Christ.[11]

Niebuhr brings to the field of Christian social ethics a
combination of realism and prophetic insight. His comment
in *Moral Man and Immoral Society* that an ethic of individual

perfection is bound to seem suspect when individuals remain embedded in unethical social structures was discussed in chapter two. We turn here to examine his positive views, as sketched in a later book, *An Interpretation of Christian Ethics.*[12]

Niebuhr sees the teaching of Jesus as a perfectionist love ethic, opening up a vertical dimension upon all man's personal and social life, but literally impossible to fulfil in the horizontal dimension of human social life. Yet in a highly creative way he urges the relevance of what he calls this 'impossible possibility' to both individual life and, more specifically, social and political life. He sees the religion of Jesus as quintessentially prophetic religion, constantly challenging men to self-criticism and change, not by direct implementation, as liberal Christianity envisaged, naively taming the ethic of Jesus and turning it into a political programme, but rather by inspiring men to take the necessary, often ambiguous and coercive steps to work for justice in the human sphere. Niebuhr insists that the realistic quest for human justice is the form which love takes in the social and economic spheres. Against the orthodox Christian tradition, he argues that the impossibility of the love ethic is not a ground for despair and conservatism in social ethics, but rather the inspiration of the determination to achieve more just human relations. And yet the presence of this vertical perfectionist dimension prevents men from resting satisfied with any particular human programme, as the Marxists do.

Niebuhr has a very sharp eye for the pathos of human perfectionism, and pinpoints the ways in which Christianity has itself again and again failed to get the relation right between the absolute ethic of Jesus and practical human possibilities; but Christianity has the resources, nevertheless, on Niebuhr's view, to provide a perspective from which both the necessity and the sinfulness of the human struggle for justice can be seen. We may illustrate Niebuhr's criticism of the tendency in Christian history to confuse the vertical and the horizontal dimensions by his comments on Luther's words to the rebellious peasants in 1525. Luther had quoted the words of Jesus, 'Resist not evil', against the German peasants, and in justification of the suppression of their revolt. Niebuhr's comment deserves quotation: 'This gratuitous introduction of the principle of non-resistance from a perfectionist ethic into a political ethic of compromise . . . creates the suspicion of a conscious adjustment to class interest. This is particularly true of Luther, because no theologian understood the impossibility of the law of love in a world of sin better than he.' Niebuhr goes on to remark of this kind of confusion in general: 'In the light of this record of orthodox Christianity to politics, the rationalistic and naturalistic rebellion against religion in the eighteenth century must be appreciated as being partly a rebellion of the ethical spirit against religious confusion.' This judgement expresses in a nutshell one of the main themes of our own first three chapters.

Niebuhr sets against this damaging tendency in Christian social ethics the prophetic spirit which does not confuse the vertical with the horizontal but brings it to bear upon the horizontal both as criticism and as inspiration – criticism of any actual human achievement, inspiration to transcend what has been achieved. Moreover he refuses to opt for a two-tier Christian ethic, such as that of the early Bonhoeffer. Like the later Bonhoeffer, he attempts to bring out the relevance of the love ethic of Jesus for the whole of life, spelling out its social implications in terms of the struggle for justice.

If we ask how Niebuhr deals with the area where it was suggested above that he was weakest, namely that of individual transformation, we must examine the chapter, entitled 'Love as a Possibility for the Individual'. We find there precisely the same pattern: recognition of the *impossibility* of unqualified love of the neighbour, together with recognition of the *possibility* of always achieving some transcendence of the limitations of natural benevolence. Moreover, Niebuhr is well aware that such transcendence cannot be willed. It is a matter of gratitude and inspiration. 'The love that cannot be willed,' he writes, 'may nevertheless grow as a natural fruit upon a tree which has its roots deep enough to be nurtured by springs of life beneath the surface and branches reaching up to heaven.' There is a hint here of an ethic of redemption, though it is doubtful whether such metaphorical language would satisfy Bonhoeffer, with his insistence on the resources of the living Christ for the Christian.

In the light of this brief examination of four leading exponents of Christian ethics in the twentieth century, let us now consider how their interpretations stand up to the criticisms of Christian ethics distinguished in previous chapters. Their social adequacy clearly varies. Niebuhr particularly and the later Bonhoeffer to a considerable extent, may be held to pass this test with flying colours and to present profound and searching versions of Christian social ethics. In a way they complement each other precisely at the point where there is some weakness or one-sidedness in each position respectively – Niebuhr being more convincing on the validity of the human struggle for justice, Bonhoeffer being more convincing on the redemptive power of Christ for Christian discipleship in the world. It should also be pointed out that Barth, for all his unwillingness to recognise the presence of God outside the covenant in human goodness and the human sense of justice, never made the kind of mistake which Luther made. His eye for the social implications of the Christian Gospel remained clear and unconfused.

There seems to be no reason at all to call in question the maturity of these interpretations of Christian ethics. Certainly they themselves show up the immaturity of some other versions of Christian moral teaching. But figures such as Kirk, Barth, Bonhoeffer and Niebuhr are a standing refutation of Freudian generalisations on this matter.

The charge of immaturity cannot be considered in isolation from that of heteronomy; for it is the burden of much secular thought since the Enlightenment that man only achieves maturity when he throws over childish relations of dependence. Here, the Christian moralist can only counter-attack and question the adequacy of this insistence on man's self-sufficiency and ethical autonomy. All four exponents of Christian ethics whom we have examined are clear that a transcendent source of human value, in relation to which man's self-estrangement is overcome and his true freedom found is the only ultimately realistic basis for bridging the gulf between fact and ideal.

The charge of intolerance is not a particularly plausible charge against any of these writers. There may be a danger of it in Barthian theology, where natural human goodness is given little independent weight, but it is interesting to discover, in the writings of a noted Barthian, Hendrik Kraemer, the following passage on the necessity of Christian tolerance: 'Real tolerance can only grow when it is fully recognised that truth can only be really obeyed in perfect spiritual freedom, because anything else or anything less is disobedience to and misunderstanding of the real character of truth.'[13]

This brings us once more to the question of truth and honesty. We have already seen that answers to the question of whether there is a transcendent source and goal of all man's good cannot be presupposed one way or the other. Either way, dogmatism tends to lead to dishonesty. But the writers examined in this chapter believed that they had perceived or been given some vision of reality. If they were right, their critics are in fundamental error about the nature of things and the sources of good. If they are wrong, then their apparent profundities must be judged illusory. But no one can seriously suppose that the issue is a trivial one.

NOTES

1. K. Kirk, *The Vision of God* (London: Longman's, 1931); *Some Principles of Moral Theology* (London: Longman's, 1920); and *Conscience and its Problems* (London: Longman's, 1927).
2. *The Vision of God* (Harper Torchbook edition), pp. 140–146.
3. J. Jeremias, New Testament Theology, Vol. I (English trans., London: SCM Press 1971), pp. 214–218.
4. An examination of the traditional opposition of divine love (agape) and earthly love (eros) might well bear this out. See J. Needham, 'Sacred and Profane Love' in *Theology* for January 1977, and the discussion of sexual ethics, pp. 89f. below.
5. The most thorough exposition and criticism of Barth's ethics is to be found in Robert E. Willis, *The Ethics of Karl Barth* (Leiden: E. J. Brill, 1971). The chapter on 'Gospel and Law' in H. Hartwell, *The Theology of Karl Barth* (London: Duckworth, 1964) may also be consulted.
6. See G. Hunsinger (ed.), *Karl Barth and Radical Politics* (English trans., Philadelphia: The Westminster Press, 1976). For critical comment on Barth's attitude to communism, see C. West, *Communism and the Theologians* (London: SCM Press, 1958).
7. R. Niebuhr, in D. B. Robertson (ed.), *Essays in Applied Christianity* (New York, Meridian Books, 1959).
8. See above p. 17.
9. *Church Dogmatics* III 2 (Edinburgh: T. & T. Clark, 1960).
10. D. Bonhoeffer, *Ethics* (English Trans., London: SCM Press, 1955).

See also *The Cost of Discipleship* (English trans., London: SCM Press, 1959). The best commentaries on Bonhoeffer's ethical writings are H. Ott, *Reality and Faith* (English trans., London: Lutterworth, 1971), chapter six, and A. Dumas, *Dietrich Bonhoeffer: Theologian of Reality* (English trans., London: SCM Press, 1971), chapters five and six.

11. See D. Bonhoeffer, *No Rusty Swords* (London: Collins, 1965), Fontana edition, pp. 109–13.
12. New York: Harper, 1935.
13. H. Kraemer, *The Christian Message in a Non-Christian World* (New York: Harper, 1935.

CHAPTER FIVE

Situation Ethics and Liberation Theology

It would be possible and interesting to continue the pattern of the last chapter by selecting a number of living exponents of Christian ethics and testing their writings for adequacy both against criticism and as providing positive moral ideals. But it would not be easy to think of such outstanding figures as the twentieth century giants just considered, and instead I intend to single out two major *trends* in contemporary Christian ethics, one of which came to the fore during the nineteen sixties and the other during the nineteen seventies.

The first of these is known as 'situation ethics' and can be characterised, according to a number of its proponents, as follows: Christian action, far from being a matter of strict obedience to rules laid down in scripture or church teaching, is determined by the application of the one basic principle of love to each particular situation as it arises. Rejection of legalism and adoption of the single principle of love are the two marks of specifically Christian ethics, according to this school. It is not suggested that rules have no place in Christian ethics. Situation ethics is not pure antinomianism. But moral rules are only rules of thumb, normal guidelines, summing up the wisdom and experience of the past, but in no sense absolute. Particular circumstances – the situation – may require them to be overridden in the name of love. Moreover this is particularly likely to be the case in times of rapid social change, such as our own, when the wisdom of the past cannot automatically be held to be appropriate to the new situation of the present.

The love which features in situation ethics as the one and only absolute is 'agape' – the Greek word used to refer to the love of God for man and to the completely other-regarding love of the Christian for his neighbour, including his enemy. It is a matter of will rather than desire; that is why it can be commanded, as it was by Jesus in his summary of the law. But, for exponents of situation ethics, Jesus' summary of the law expresses the whole of the law, the real heart and spirit of the divine command which relativises every other ordinance. A much quoted example is Jesus' commendation of David, who, when he and his men were hungry, took and ate the holy bread from the temple, which was strictly forbidden to any but the priests.

Moreover there can be no conflict, according to situation ethics, between love and justice; for justice *is* love distributed fairly. The 'situation' includes all who are affected by the act, and anyone acting out of love will aim to do what he can to maximise the well-being of all concerned, and certainly not just that of one or the few at the expense of others. Love as justice, then, is the basis of Christian social ethics, according to this school.

An immediate reaction, on being confronted with this modern version of Christian ethics, is suspicion that far too much weight is being put on the individual's ability to read the situation aright and to determine what is the most 'agapeistic' thing to do, let alone actually to do it. But this objection can be met, and is met, by a combination of two considerations.

First, it is stressed that the Christian does not read situations and act in them as an isolated individual anyway. He judges and acts as a member of the Church, as one of a body committed to 'agapeistic' action. Secondly, he does not judge and act out of human resources alone. The point of specifically Christian life and action is that it is, or should be, sustained and enabled by divine resources, by the grace and inspiration of the God who *is* Love.[1]

The more we think about Christian situation ethics, thus interpreted, the more we may be inclined to suppose that it does indeed capture the heart of Christian ethics. Much of the reaction of Jesus and Paul against the legalism of the Judaism of their day can be understood in this light. Even Blanshard, prior to his criticism of the teaching of Jesus, allows that a salient characteristic of the ethics of Jesus was the attempt to reconstruct men's attitudes, rather than to lay down rules of behaviour. Further, Blanshard observes that Jesus 'was the tactitian, not the strategist of charity, dealing with each case as it arose.' One could scarcely find a more succinct way of expressing the central affirmations of situation ethics. Moreover, there are definite 'situationist' elements in each of the four exponents of Christian ethics whom we considered in the previous chapter. For all his emphasis on moral principles and casuistry, Kirk insisted in *The Vision of God* that the aim of Christian ethics was growth into personal union with Christ such as to leave the need for rules behind. It will also be recalled that Barth's insistence on obedience to the divine command, far from taking a legalistic form, was expressed in terms of an uncompromising 'actualism', whereby the Christian, in his particular situation, is confronted by the will and command of the living God. Indeed Barth's 'actualism' is one of the theological sources of Christian situation ethics. The

85

later Bonhoeffer's position was not dissimilar, and his own judgement and action in the unprecedented situation of Nazi Germany have become a standard example for later situation ethics in the sphere of social and political responsibility. The central theme of Niebuhr's interpretation of Christian ethics is also the bearing of the perfectionist love ethic of Jesus on the 'horizontal' concrete situations of interpersonal, social and political life.

It can also be argued that Christian situation ethics is well placed to meet the criticisms listed earlier. It is in no sense a prudential ethic; its love principle is utterly disinterested. There is no arbitrary heteronomy either in its understanding of the will of God or in its attitude to Church tradition and moral rules. Each man must act according to his own judgement in the situation, though, of course, the judgement of a Christian situationist will be informed about and open to the ultimate context of the divine love. Further, there is room, according to this ethic, for growth into mature perception of man's true end and of what makes for his ultimate well-being. Christian action, inspired by love, in response to the particular situation, represents the authentic freedom of the Christian man. And, as we have seen, the conception of love as justice is held to meet the requirement for a viable social ethic.

Notwithstanding these positive features, including these constructive ways of meeting the critics of traditional Christian ethics, situation ethics has itself met with considerable criticism from Christian moral theologians. Here we must remember the other problem mentioned at the beginning of this book as to whether a particular suggested version of Christian ethics can reasonably be held to be authentically Christian.

One criticism has already been dealt with. The accusation

of subjectivism and individualism can be met by stressing the Church context of Christian decision – the corporate nature of the living spirituality which forms the context of specifically Christian action. But other criticisms are less easily met. Even when a man is acting as a member of the Church, he cannot easily treat each situation as an independent, intelligible unit with its own unique claims. Moral principles and general norms of right and wrong help to define a situation for what it is. Moreover a person becomes a moral agent as he learns to act consistently in accordance with general rules. The situationist may reply that the only rule required, both for consistent moral action and for recognition of what each situation demands, is the rule of love. But here we meet with the main criticism of situation ethics. It was expressed tersely by the Roman Catholic moral theologian, Bernard Häring, when he wrote of one situationist's views that his 'concept of love is structureless'.[2] The argument is that love must be spelled out in terms of more detailed norms, such as have characterised traditional codes of right and wrong, if it is to assess situations and guide action aright. Certainly the rules are meant to serve love. Love is their ultimate justification. And love may, in very exceptional circumstances justify the breaking of rules. But it is naive to think that one can always appeal straight to love or pile up exception upon exception. There is clearly some force in this criticism.

Let us examine the pros and cons of situation ethics a little further by taking two examples, those of medical ethics and of sexual ethics.

A strong case can be made for the view that in medical ethics we cannot rely on the one absolute principle of love alone. The complexity and seriousness of the issues of life and death, which are part of the day to day work of doctors and nurses in a large hospital preclude the possibility of referring each decision directly to the ultimate love principle. Admittedly, Gordon Dunstan's remark that 'compassion could destroy a potentially good nurse in a week'[3] misses the point, since, as we have already indicated, the love of which situation ethics speaks is not a matter of sentiment but of will. But hard-pressed medical staff undoubtedly require a much more specific professional code of practice based on much more specific rules, such as that forbidding euthanasia, if they are not to be reduced to inaction by the sheer difficulty of decision in particular cases. Moreover it is essential to the relationship of trust between doctor and patient that such a rule should be known to obtain. This shows, incidentally, that such a rule does indeed serve love, though its point would be lost if that had to be established each time. On the other hand it is also undoubtedly the case that there may come a time when in particular circumstances, say, a life-support machine will be switched off or a lethal dose (or series of doses) of morphine administered. Such decisions are made and may well have to be made. To the situationist, this shows that the rules and codes of practice are not absolute, in the way in which the love principle is absolute. For it is the love principle which guides the exceptional act. Are we then reduced to saying that the difference between the traditionalist and the situationist is that the former stresses the need for rules, while the latter stresses the possibility of exceptions? It does seem to be true that, if the possibility of exceptions is conceded at all, then the situationist's position is in principle justified, even if we may still wish to criticise his preoccupation with exceptions and his naivety in supposing that each case can be decided by appeal to the love principle alone.

One of the factors supporting the need for rules and codes

of practice in medical ethics is the ever present possibility of some particular interest coming surreptitiously to influence a decision supposedly made in the light of love alone. This is an even more blatant problem in the field of sexual ethics. For here we *are* dealing with love in the sense of sentiment and desire as well as that of concern for the well-being of the other. The relation of 'eros' and 'agape' greatly complicates the matter. The traditionalist will urge that this factor reinforces the need for moral rules governing relations between the sexes, and that it is naive and unrealistic to suppose that sexual behaviour can be regulated by appeal to agape alone. On the other hand the situationist may well point out that the purpose of such rules in restricting sexual relations to a context of agape as well as of eros is forgotten when the rules are turned into absolutes and ends in themselves. He will not find it hard to produce examples from real life or from fiction where in the circumstances extra-marital sex (to say nothing of divorce) seems to be justified by the ultimate love (agape) principle. Moreover the facts about sexual relations clearly change with the introduction of reliable methods of contraception.

How are we to evaluate this dispute, bearing in mind the fact that secular critics of Christian ethics such as Russell and Kahl have been loud in their condemnation of traditional Christian attitudes to these matters? Certainly, in Christian ethics today, we shall need to take a much more positive view of 'eros' as part of God's good creation than was taken in earlier Christian centuries. (We may well at this point wish to question the situationists' own rigid separation between 'eros' and 'agape'.[4]) Certainly, too, we shall need to argue the case for limiting full sexual activity to contexts of genuine love and commitment, if human beings are to be treated as persons and not just as objects of desire. Moreover, no more than in medical ethics, shall we be persuaded by production of a series of extraordinary exceptional cases that the traditional rules are no longer required or that these matters can be left to individual judgement in the light of agape alone. On the other hand we may perhaps agree with the situationists that less rigid attitudes to homosexuality[5] and to divorce are required in Christian ethics today, and that, notwithstanding the necessary norms governing sexual relations, there may be *occasional* exceptional circumstances for which no legislation or convention will be adequate.

So far I have expressed some guarded sympathy with situation ethics, as an important, if somewhat exaggerated, trend in Christian ethics today, and one which has some claim to meet the criteria of disinterestedness, relative autonomy and maturity that we have accepted, with qualification, from secular criticism. But we must return now to the question of social adequacy; for the situationists' equation of love and justice has not persuaded critics that they have a sufficient basis, in the one ultimate love principle, for a viable social ethic in the modern world. The criticism has been pressed in ecumenical circles (especially in conferences of the World Council of Churches) that, with its emphasis on circumstances deciding cases, situation ethics is 'in danger of being manipulated and controlled by circumstances and events'.[6] The point is akin to Häring's basic criticism of situation ethics. Love as justice is too structureless a concept to guide action in social and political conflict, and in particular to enable us to stand out against the pressure of circumstances making for accommodation and compromise. This brings us to the other trend in contemporary Christian ethics to be considered in this chapter, namely, liberation theology, and I shall postpone evaluation of this criticism of situation ethics until liberation theology has been examined.

Liberation theology is an attempt to spell out the social and political implications of the Christian gospel in terms of the liberation of men and women from oppression and injustice. It rejects any interpretation of Christian ethics in either individualist or otherworldly terms, and it denounces much previous Christian political involvement as legitimation of the status quo and betrayal of the message of the Bible.[7] Appeal is made to the Old Testament, to the God of the Exodus, who led His people out from bondage, to the Judaeo-Christian conception of God as active in history, to the Christian doctrines of incarnation, resurrection and redemption as all endorsing and demanding much more than conversion of individuals. The implication of these doctrines, it is held, is that God is at work in the world to change man's total situation – in the words of the Magnificat 'He hath put down the mighty from their seat and hath exalted the humble and meek; he hath filled the hungry with good things and the rich he hath sent empty away.' In fact these theologians spell out the more specifically Christian ideal of love of the enemy in terms of the liberation not only of the oppressed, but also of the oppressors from themselves.

This theologically based insistence on the implications of Christian social ethics for social and political transformation or even revolution has, not surprisingly, come from Latin America where Roman Catholics are concerned, and from Africa where Protestant theology and the World Council of Churches are concerned, though it has also found considerable support from German and American theologians. It is a marked feature of the shift in the centre of gravity of world Christianity from the old established Churches of Europe and

91

the United States to the newer Churches of the 'third world'. It is, in other words, a response by Christians, out of a changed Church 'context', to the rapidly changing 'situation' of the poor in the developing countries of today.

We can scarcely quarrel with liberation theology for its attempt to spell out the political implications of Christianity. Throughout this book we have seen that one of the strongest points of criticism against traditional Christian ethics has been its failure to take seriously the social and political aspects of love of the neighbour. We have also seen how Barth, Bonhoeffer and Niebuhr were all constrained, out of faithfulness to the biblical conception of the Kingdom of God, to redress this imbalance and to insist that Christians and the Church be committed to the struggle for human justice. Doubts arise not over the necessity for political commitment nor over the emphasis on justice, but rather over the precise analyses of the contemporary situation offered and over the means considered permissible for bringing about liberation.

I have stressed the strong theological basis of liberation theology; but it is also true that these authors are considerably influenced by Marxism, and it has been suggested that the latter is the real source of their political commitment and that the theology has been tailored to fit the Marxist standpoint. This thesis, put forward by the 1978 Reith Lecturer,[8] fails to do justice to the powerful theological arguments of writers such as Gutierrez and Moltmann, and also overlooks the possibility that a Marxist analysis of the situation to which this theology is applied may actually be correct. Throughout the history of Christianity, in both its theoretical and its practical aspects, Christian theology has found it necessary to relate to current philosophical understanding, be it Platonist, Aristotelian, Kantian or Marxist. And if our initial statement of the relation between theological and secular thought was right, we should expect to find some valid insight on the part of secular thought into the structures of human life and into what makes for human well-being. We have ourselves, following Niebuhr, accepted criticism from Marxism of some aspects of traditional Christianity, notably its connivance in unjust social structures. But we have also criticised Marxism for its utopianism, its neglect of the problem of abuse of power and its tendency towards totalitarianism. We shall want to question liberation theology, in so far as it embraces a Marxist analysis of the situation, as to whether it has adequately reckoned with these problems. It may be, too, that we shall wish to disagree with the Marxist analysis of the situation in developing countries. It may be that we shall wish to press the case for development and reform rather than for revolution, though it is easier to say this from a European standpoint than from an African or Latin American one. Equally, it is easier for the European, who is not confronted so sharply with the 'unacceptable face of capitalism' as are the poor in the third world, to counsel patience and to warn against inflated expectations.

All this goes to show that, just as situation ethics overestimates the ease with which the moral situation can be identified and assessed, so liberation theology may too easily endorse a Marxist analysis of the oppressed state of the poor.

Critics have also questioned the actual *theology* of liberation. In particular the equation of redemption and liberation has been held to obfuscate the relation of the individual to the group. It neglects the facts that a man can be redeemed even though he remains politically in bondage and that men can be liberated politically without being redeemed. Christian ethics cannot ignore this lack of equivalence. But liberation theology at its best is perfectly aware of this.

The other main problem with liberation theology is the problem of means – to be more precise, the problem of violent means. The chief criticism of liberation theology has been over its willingness to give moral support to violent revolution or guerrilla warfare, and occasionally to participate in it, where it seems that no other way can be expected to bring about the liberation of the oppressed. The influence of Marxism on Christian ethics is even more blatant here, and it seems, at first sight to be diametrically opposed to the teaching and practice of Jesus and to the whole spirit of Christian ethics. Jesus taught men to overcome evil with good, and himself trod the way of the Cross rather than espouse the Zealot cause of violent revolution against the Roman occupation.[9] And indeed the mainspring of Christian ethics, as we have seen, has been disinterested love, including love of the enemy, forgiveness and reconciliation. How then can Christians even think of supporting violent revolution? The question is not so easy to answer as might appear. Only if the ethic of Jesus is held to entail absolute pacifism can an unequivocal no to force or violence (the words are synonymous) be maintained. It should be pointed out that a number of leading Latin American liberation theologians *are* pacifists and reject violence without qualification. On the other hand the mainstream Christian Churches have never committed themselves without reserve to pacifism. Notwithstanding their recognition of the primacy of love and forgiveness, and their rejection of hatred and revenge, they have not believed it right to apply the command of Jesus, Resist not evil, directly to political and international life. The Thomist tradition has held that, if the just war was permissible, the just rebellion against tyrrany was permissible too.[10] We have seen both aspects of this in Bonhoeffer's ethics. For all his literal insistence, in *The Cost of Discipleship* on obedience to the teaching of Jesus in the Sermon on the Mount, he did not believe that the command, 'Resist not evil', could or should be applied directly to the state. And in his last years he came to believe it his Christian duty actively to support the plot to assassinate Hitler.

The ethical ambiguities of both war and revolution are very great. In neither case should we expect Christians, still less the Church, to give uncritical support. Church enthusiasm for war in 1914 now looks like betrayal of Christianity. Conversely the restraint urged by Bishop Bell on the means contemplated and used in the Second World War is an example of eminently Christian witness in the face of British enthusiasm for 'unconditional surrender'. Similarly we would look for Christian voices to be urging restraint and reconciliation in and after revolutionary situations. We cannot countenance any resort to the language of the 'holy war', found most strikingly in the Crusades and in Islam today. Where Christian revolutionaries, however just their cause, resort to such sanctification of violence, we may be sure that they have parted company with the spirit as well as the letter of the ethics of Jesus.

If we now return to the question whether liberation theology has taken Christian social ethics much further than has situation ethics, the answer must be mainly negative. Liberation theology may be read as an instance of situation ethics in the social and political sphere, open to the same reservations and the same guarded support that we gave to situation ethics in general. Its basic principle is love as justice, and there is no more and no less danger of situation ethics 'being manipu-

lated and controlled by circumstances' than there is of liberation theology's being manipulated and controlled by
Marxism. Situation ethics and liberation theology alike require both sound theological judgement and practical wisdom
in face of the complexities of modern political and economic
conditions – theological judgement in remaining faithful to
basic Christian doctrines and to the ideal of justice, practical
wisdom in reading the situation aright and working realisti-
cally for the liberation of the poor and the oppressed.

It follows from this assimilation of liberation theology to
situation ethics that we shall make the same replies to our
critics of Christian ethics on the scores of disinterestedness,
autonomy, maturity and scope as we made before; and in
addition we shall stress that this development in Christian
ethics shows something of Christian theology's ability to de-
rive a social ethic from its fundamental doctrines and values.
It is far from clear that Christianity today – especially on a
world scale – is vulnerable to the strictures of Kahl.

It may well be that our critics will reply that these contemporary versions of Christian ethics have come too far from
their origins in the teaching of Jesus to count as authentic
representations of Christian ethics. It will be recalled that
Kaufmann refused to accept even Niebuhr's work as a genuine
interpretation of Christian ethics for this very reason. Many
Christians will doubtless share this suspicion. But we should
recall also Blanshard's recognition that Jesus himself was concerned primarily with attitudes and with dealing with each
case as it arose. The critic cannot have his cake and eat it.
Critics of Christian ethics must take the subject as they find
it; and it can hardly be denied that, simply as a matter of
phenomenology, the figures and trends which we have been
considering in this and the previous chapter exemplify Christ-

ian ethics today. If the theological basis of these versions can be made out, and if the results can be shown to give some claim to adequacy and indeed to constructive ethical insight, then these must be the issues in debate, and not some frozen picture from the past.

Kahl's other question about that past must not be forgotten. What does it mean, he asked, that the religion which speaks of love has actually perpetrated the horrors of the Inquisition and the Crusades in the course of history? Christians may ask to be judged by Christian ethics at its best, but what are they to say about these failures and perversions down the centuries? Is it enough to speak of man's inveterate tendency to corrupt even the best? Christians *can* cry 'tu quoque'. They *can* ask, What does it mean that Marxist-Leninist idealism has led to Stalin's purges and the horrors documented by Solzhenitsyn? They *can* even suggest that Marxism today shows far less sign of having repented of its past inhumanities than does Christianity today. But there is no easy answer to Kahl's question. All that can be said is that the horrors of the past must not be permitted to destroy or to minimise perception of the ultimate nature and destiny of man. If Christianity, properly understood, in fact reveals God's will for human life and human community, and provides the spiritual resources by which man, in both his individual and communal life, can be transformed, then past corruptions cannot falsify those basic truths. The view of Kahl that it is dishonest to attribute Christian saintliness and brotherhood to the grace of God and Christian cruelty and intolerance to human weakness and perversity may simply be mistaken. That differentiation may in fact correspond to the realities of the case. We know that man has it in him to abuse his best intentions. It may be that he does *not* have the power to realise the good without God's grace and inspiration. It is also clear that God does not forcibly fulfil His purposes. His grace works patiently and at great cost through recalcitrant human media. But if He is indeed the ultimate source of all good, there is no dishonesty in men and women coming to acknowledge it.

The treatment of Christian social ethics in this chapter and in this book as a whole, with its emphasis on justice, its sensitivity to Marxist criticism, and its positive assessment of Barth, Niebuhr and the theology of liberation, may be felt by some to have been biased towards the view that socialist policies alone are compatible with the Christian gospel. Certainly Barth in his early days went too far in saying that 'socialism is a predicate of the gospel'. Particular political creeds are too ambiguous and transitory to be endorsed without qualification or criticism by Christian theology. The vertical dimension must not be conflated with the horizontal. But theological judgement must be linked to a realistic appraisal of human needs, and, while Christians may differ in their reading of the facts, there must be some limit to permissible Christian assessments of the situation. For example, a more organic view of human community may predispose the Christian to adopt relatively conservative policies. It should be recalled that Niebuhr himself in later years moved some way towards a conservative position. But a racist reading of the human situation, or one which explicitly endorses the exploitation of one segment of mankind by another, must, on any view, be regarded as incompatible with the Christian gospel. On balance it may be said that the ideals of socialism are most readily embraced by Christians on theological grounds, especially when the theology is ecumenical in nature and when it focuses on the world community. This is why the Christian mind is inclined to hold that communism errs in the right direction, while fascism errs in the wrong direction. On the other hand, the limits of what can be achieved politically should also be borne in mind. Bonhoeffer held, with the Lutheran tradition, that the role of government is 'regulative' rather than 'constitutive'. The most it can do is to ensure just conditions. It cannot constitute human community as such. If this view is right, we have another reason for refusing unqualified support to socialism, especially when it acquires utopian overtones.

NOTES

1. Typical expositions of situation ethics are J. Fletcher, *Situation Ethics* (London: SCM Press, 1966) and J. A. T. Robinson, *Christian Morals Today* (London: SCM Press, 1965). Stress on the Church context of Christian action is to be found in P. Lehmann, *Ethics in a Christian Context* (New York: Harper and Row, 1963). For criticism of situation ethics, see J. Macquarrie, *Three Issues in Ethics* (London: SCM Press, 1970) and G. F. Woods, 'Situational Ethics', in I. T. Ramsey (ed.), *Christian Ethics and Contemporary Philosophy* (London: SCM Press, 1966).
2. B. Häring, *Shalom: Peace* (English trans., New York: Farrar, Straus and Giroux, 1968), p. 47.
3. G. Dunstan, The Artifice of Ethics (London: SCM Press, 1974), p. 13.
4. See the reference to J. Needham's article, in note 4 to chapter four.
5. Christian ethics, like any other ethics, must surely distinguish between promiscuous homosexuality and a stable homosexual relationship.
6. E. de Vries, 'The Background of the Text in Ecumenical Ethics', in R. H. Preston (ed.), *Technology and Social Justice* (London: SCM Press, 1971), p. 42.
7. A classic of liberation theology is G. Gutierrez, *A Theology of Liberation* (English trans, New York: Orbis Books, 1973, and London: SCM Press 1974). See also the three books by J. Moltmann: *Theology of Hope* (English trans., London: SCM Press, 1967), *The Crucified God* (English trans., London: SCM Press, 1974) and *The Church in the*

Power of the Spirit (English trans., London: SCM Press, 1977). For comment, see A. Dumas, *Political Theology and the Life of the Church* (English trans., London: SCM Press, 1978).

8. See note 11 to chapter three. For criticism, see M. Dummett's lecture: 'Catholicism and the World Order', published by the Catholic Institute for International Relations, London, 1979.
9. See M. Hengel, *Victory over Violence* (English trans., Philadelphia: The Fortress Press, 1973, and London: SPCK, 1975).
10. See J. G. Davies, *Christians, Politics and Violent Revolution* (London: SCM Press, 1976).

CHAPTER SIX

Christian Ethics and the Religions of the World

Our investigations into both secular criticism and the adequacy of Christian ethics have been restricted to the sphere of historical and contemporary Christianity. So far nothing has been said about the fact that other world religions also contain profound ethical teaching, sometimes apparently in harmony, but sometimes apparently conflicting with Christian ethics. Any defence of the adequacy of Christian ethics must reckon with the fact of these different ultimate religious values, and moreover with rival conceptions of the spiritual resources available to men and women for the realisation of those values.

Until relatively recently, the superiority of Christianity as an ethical system was assumed by Christians. Just as the reality and power of secular ethics were widely denied and the idea of morality without religion regarded as dangerously subversive, so the ethical content of other faiths was overlooked and Christianity held to bring not only the gospel but morality as well to the heathen. The study of religions on a comparative basis soon revealed the implausibility of this view, at least to the world of scholarship. Theologians could no longer deny the fact of other systems of religious ethics. But even the highly sophisticated missionary theologian, Hendrik Kraemer, whose remarks on tolerance were quoted approvingly in chapter four, could still assert: 'The Christian ethic . . . is entirely incommensurable with all other ethics in the world.' 'All ethics in the world except the Christian ethic, are some form of eudaemonism'.[1] Eudaemonism is the view that the value of moral action lies in its capacity to produce happiness. For Kraemer, Christianity and Christianity alone teaches the love of God and of the neighbour, irrespective of any other motive. This was of course the view of a pronounced Barthian, but liberal Christianity too, well into the mid-twentieth century, was attempting to argue for at least the relative superiority of Christian ethics. The father of liberal Christianity, Friedrich Schleiermacher (1768–1834), in his great work of systematic theology, *The Christian Faith*,[2] has a fascinating short section, in which, having argued in favour of monotheism over all forms of polytheism, fetishism and pantheism, on the grounds of monotheism's superior ability to foster the sense of absolute dependence, he goes on to express an equally quick preference for 'teleological' religion, which subordinates the natural to the moral, over 'aesthetic' religion, which subordinates the moral to the natural. Since he recognised only Christianity, Judaism and 'Mohammedanism' as monotheistic faiths, and claimed to see in the latter's fatalism an expression of the aesthetic type, this left him with Christianity and 'less perfectly' Judaism. His reason for this last judgement, interestingly, is that Judaism relates its 'God-consciousness' to reward and punishment rather than to moral challenge. Thus Schleiermacher swiftly arrives at the conclusion of Christianity's superiority on ethical as much as religious grounds.

There is a similar passage in the turn of the century German theologian, Ernst Troeltsch (1865–1923), who was known as the systematic theologian of the 'history of religions school'.[3]

Having dismissed polytheism as of interest only to the student of the origins of religion, Troeltsch proceeds to distinguish between the religions of law and the religions of redemption. The former, Judaism and Islam – according to Troeltsch – fail to overcome the divide between the natural and the transcendent world. This leaves only Christianity and the Indian religions as religions of redemption. Troeltsch has a very interesting discussion of Hinduism and Buddhism, but says at the end: 'It is necessary to make a choice between redemption through meditation on Transcendent Being or Non-Being and redemption through faithful, trusting participation in the person-like character of God, the ground of all life and of all genuine value . . . The higher goal and the greater profundity of life are found on the side of the personalistic religion.' Thus, on somewhat different grounds, and via a different process of selection, Troeltsch reaches the same conclusion as does Schleiermacher. Even Niebuhr generalises in much the same way. He recognises the presence of a love ideal in Buddhism, for instance, but argues that prophetic religion is better able to foster a dynamic love-ethic than a passionless otherworldliness. Buddhism, on Niebuhr's view, is 'unable to escape an enervating ambiguity in its statement of the love ideal'.[4]

Such broad generalisations may be preferable to blanket condemnations of other religions on account of particular malpractices which they may have fostered or tolerated at certain stages in their history, such as the practice of 'sati' – the immolation of widows on their husband's funeral pyres – in Hinduism. (Such a condemnation would be strictly parallel to the condemnation of Christianity on account of the burning of witches in the seventeenth century.) They are preferable too to such theologically weighted judgements as

103

that of the Anglican Article Thirteen, which observes that 'works done before the grace of Christ are not pleasant to God . . . and have the nature of sin', or indeed to Kraemer's more sophisticated judgement that all non-Christian ethics are eudaimonistic. But even the liberal theologian's *arguments* for the superiority of Christian ethics are much too general and superficial to satisfy the student of comparative religion. In the first place, they rely on very monolithic notions of both Christianity and other faiths. They fail to do justice to the heights and depths of all religions, including Christianity. And, secondly, such judgements fail to reckon with the resources of other faiths for development and reformation.

Often a secular critic will turn out to be more just in his assessment of a religion such as Buddhism. We have already noted Kaufmann's preference for Buddhist ethics over Christian ethics. A less positive, but very perceptive judgement is given by the American philosopher, A. C. Danto.[5] He points out that the moral ideals enshrined in the Buddha's teaching of the Noble Eightfold Path require the complete dedication of the life of the Buddhist monk, and themselves culminate in the more mystical teaching about enlightenment and release into nirvana. Indeed the strength of Theravada Buddhism (the form believed to be closest to the Buddha's original teaching) lies in the monastic community, the Sangha. 'To the layman', writes Danto, 'Buddhism has little to offer beyond the conventional homilies.' And he goes on to point out that, even in the developed forms of Mahayana Buddhism, the 'bodhisattva' ideal, whereby the Buddhist saint postpones his own enlightenment out of compassion for the unenlightened, is still a disproportionate ideal, far beyond the capacities of the ordinary layman.

It would be interesting to compare this secular criticism of

Buddhism with the secular criticisms of Christianity which have preoccupied us in this book. We should also expect to find Buddhist scholars replying to this criticism in ways comparable to those in which exponents of Christian ethics reply to criticisms of Christian perfectionism. We notice the same problem of the gap between reality and ideal arising in the Buddhist context as concerned Bonhoeffer in his treatment of Christian ethics.

Danto's chief criticism of Buddhism, as of other oriental ethical systems, has yet to be mentioned. It rests on his philosophical conviction that the adequacy of any moral teaching stands or falls by the truth or falsity of its factual beliefs about man and the world. Thus it is the truth or falsity of the Buddha's diagnosis of the human predicament and of his purported discernment of the spiritual resources available to man to overcome his universal involvement in the craving that makes for suffering that will decide the issue for or against the Buddhist way. Again we note the similarity between this criticism and those of Russell, Flew and Robinson concerning what they held to be the falsity of Christian belief.

While we may agree that the question of the truth or falsity of the related religious doctrines is important for our assessment of religious ethics, and while we may insist against the critics that these questions of truth are open and serious questions, not to be pre-judged either way, the actual qualities and ideals exemplified and taught in the religions are likely to weigh just as much, if not more, with the impartial student of religious ethics. For this reason, let us pursue a little further the nature and potentialities of the Buddhist moral teaching, as an example of comparative religious ethics.

Compassion is one of the most notable features of Buddhism. Comparative ethics will certainly involve the fullest study

105

of the way in which it comes to expression in the 'bodhisattva' ideal of Mahayana Buddhism, and of the way it can be both compared and contrasted with Christian love (agape). Buddhist compassion is illustrated by the well-known story of the bodhisattva and the hungry tigress: the bodhisattva, out of compassion for suffering beings in the world, gives his own body for food to a tigress and her cubs about to starve to death. The story no doubt impresses; but the critic will question its implied equation of animal and human suffering. He will further question the context of the story in which this act of deep compassion is' itself seen as a way to incomparably wonderful enlightenment. We are reminded of criticisms of the allegedly prudential motivation of the Christian love ethic, and would wish to discover whether a comparable answer can be given in the Buddhist case. No doubt it can; for we find a much more altruistic strand in the Zen-Buddhist, Suzuki's saying, praised by Kaufmann, that if he believed in heaven and hell, he would certainly refuse to go to heaven and insist on going to hell to share the suffering of the damned. Christian comment on this notion of utterly disinterested self-sacrifice will doubtless follow Kirk in questioning the ideal of self-sacrifice for its own sake. This saying of Suzuki's will be contrasted with the attitude of the third century Church father, Origen, summarised by John Robinson as follows: 'Christ remains on the cross so long as the last sinner remains in hell.'[6] The implication of this Christian universalism is that self-sacrifice is not an end in itself, but can be expected to achieve some ultimate reconciliation.

A comparable idea, too, is found in Buddhism in the statement of the bodhisattva's resolve to take upon himself the burden of all suffering: 'It is surely better that I alone should be in pain than that all these being should fall into the states of woe. Therefore I must give myself away as a pawn through which the whole world is redeemed from the terror of the hells . . .'[7] The question now arises how it is envisaged that this transference is effected; and there may be difficulties here for the Buddhist comparable to those which have perplexed Christian theology over the mechanics of Atonement. And before long the dialogue will have led to the question of the different conceptions of the ultimate destiny of man. All this illustrates Danto's point about the connection between ethical ideals and doctrines. For we are not just comparing human moral attitudes and ideals. In earlier chapters, the problem was noted of the gap between reality and ideal, where all forms of morality were concerned. The doctrines of the religions attempt to delineate the ways in which that gap can be bridged. As Danto recognises, much depends on the truth or falsity of those doctrines. Kaufmann praises Buddhism for providing men and women with 'a humanitarian ethic that does not depend upon special ideas about God's nature'. But the Buddhist ethic is bound up with other doctrines, and the question still remains whether in fact the possibilities of human goodness *are* in the end determined by God's nature.

We are now involved in a dialogue situation of some complexity. Recognition of the interconnection of doctrine and ethics involves the representatives of each religion in many-sided conversations over the truth-claims of each other's faith. Moreover the secular critic will always constitute a 'third partner' in a dialogue between representatives of any two religions. He may, for example, endorse the Hindu or Buddhist criticism of the Christian concept of sin on account of the sense of guilt with it often fosters in people. The secular critic may well prefer the Hindu and Buddhist teaching that man's predicament is one of ignorance rather than sin. As we have seen, in consideration of Freud's criticism, Christians can develop excessive and destructive guilt complexes. Christian moral theologians have themselves become self-critical on this score, and concerned to guard against the cultivation of an unreasonable sense of sin. But the question of sin and guilt is ultimately bound up with a proper evaluation of moral responsibility in inter-personal relations both at the human level and in respect of a man's relation with his God. Here again, doctrine and ethics are inextricable. The secular critic may be asked to note especially that the primacy of the personal is at stake. The Christian apologist may argue that the Indian stress on ignorance rather than sin is bound up with the tendency at least, in some prominent strands of Indian religion, to regard the personal as a subordinate, lower level, manifestation, of no ultimate significance.

The secular critic of Buddhist ethics will also wish to press the same criticism of social inadequacy as was made against Christian ethics. Buddhist social teaching although it has contributed to stable family and political life for many centuries in Buddhist lands has been of a somewhat conventional and conservative kind. It has always been transcended by the monastic ideal and the higher possibility of individual enlightenment and release into nirvana. Similarly western critics have often felt that Hinduism lacks the resources for a dynamic and creative social ethic. The pervasive belief in 'karma', the accumulation of the consequences of good and bad actions in a succession of reincarnations, certainly encourages a man to live in such a way as to accumulate better karma, but it also tends to encourage the view that other men's suffering must be due to 'bad karma' from previous lives. This sense of suffering as always being just can militate against an active social concern. Again, the pervasive notion of 'dharma' ('duty', or even, as it is sometimes translated, 'religion') is closely tied to the rigid caste system that still inhibits social progress in India today.

On the other hand, justice must be done to the potentialities for development in any great religion that has sustained the faith of millions down the centuries. It is interesting to observe the developments of Buddhism in Sri Lanka (Ceylon), for example. It had always been taught that the people should give alms to the Sangha – the community of Buddhist monks. It is now being taught that this duty, enjoined by the Buddha himself, may be fulfilled by giving money for hospitals and social services. Similar reinterpretations of Hindu teaching characterise the reform movements of modern Hinduism, such as that of Swami Vivekananda (1863–1902) and the Ramakrishna Mission which he founded, and which has fostered social work and awakened social conscience throughout India. For all his indebtedness to the Sermon on the Mount, Mahatma Gandhi (1869–1948) remained a Hindu and found in the pervasive Indian doctrine of 'ahimsa' (non-violence) the basis for his powerful notion of 'soul-force', by which he successfully inspired the Indian people's struggle for national liberation, and by which he sought, admittedly less successfully, to overcome the caste system and the hostility between Hindu and Muslim in the sub-continent.

It is sometimes said that these developments in Buddhism and Hinduism have arisen out of the encounter with Christianity and Western social ethics, especially in the nineteenth century. This is much too grudging an argument. Even if this view has some historical truth, it is clear by now that the encounter with the west has led to the discovery of the social ethical potentialities of the Indian tradition itself and of its capacity for internal renaissance. It is as open to the modern

Buddhist or Hindu to interpret this social teaching and activity as a discovery of essential Buddhist or Hindu meaning as it is for the modern Christian to interpret Christian social ethics as a discovery of essential Christian meaning.

Whether these faiths have the ability to meet the more radical Marxist criticisms is another matter. In many Buddhist lands, at least, religious life and culture have been overridden by Marxist revolution in ways which have appalled the civilised world.

The feature of the Indian religions which has caused most disquiet to western minds, both secular and religious, is the apparent tendency to place the ethical at a lower level of significance than the mystical. This question of the place of the ethical is an important question for the evaluation of any religion, and we shall examine it with respect to Christianity in the next chapter of this book. But the problem is a particularly difficult one for the Indian religions, not only because they tend to relegate ethical duties to the level of 'penultimate' concern, but because they tend to go even further and speak of certain states or ideals as beyond good and evil.

In the first place ethical duties seem only to have a relative significance. It has always been the Hindu ideal for a man, when he has fulfilled his duties as a householder and a father, to leave home in order to wander in the forest as an ascetic in search of 'moksha' (release, or liberation). Similarly, the Buddhist ideal, however qualified, as in Mahayana teaching, by compassion, is of a higher quest for enlightenment and release into nirvana. But at times the Hindu scriptures praise the mystical state in terms transcending ethical categories altogether. The ultimately non-personal, undifferentiated nature of the final destiny of man can have this effect not only of relativising but of annulling ethical distinctions. To think

110

of the highest state as beyond good and evil cannot but devalue the ethical. The point is made by Ninian Smart in an imaginary inter-religious dialogue, when he makes the Christian representative insist that it is appropriate to say that God is beyond good because He is supremely good, not because he is beyond good and evil. Religion, it is argued, gives substance to moral idealism and though God's moral transcendence makes men question their own ideals and achievements, it must be held that God exceeds or transcends goodness in the direction of greater goodness, not that He is beyond good and evil.[8]

The idea of something 'beyond good and evil' has Nietzschean overtones to the western mind. It is clear, however, that the mystical states of absorbtion into the absolute or isolation from the wheel of rebirth are not intended in Indian religion to negate values such as compassion and non-violence. Such an inference has been drawn, in a sharp and somewhat unbalanced way, by the late Professor R. C. Zaehner in the last of his published works, *Our Savage God*.[9] Zaehner quotes the Katha Upanishad:

> Should the killer think: 'I kill',
> Or the killed, 'I have been killed',
> Both these have no right knowledge,
> He does not kill nor is he killed.

This transcendence of ordinary awareness of action and passion is held by Zaehner to have characterised precisely the state of mind of the Californian mass murderer, Charles Manson. But such an abuse of Indian spirituality no more captures the essence of Hinduism than the racialist theology of the 'German Christians' under Hitler captured the essence of Christianity. But the critic does not have to go to the extremes of Zaehner's interpretation to retain some sense of uneasiness at the ethical implications of belief in the ultimate transcendence of all distinctions. Even the Hindu devotional scripture, the Bhagavadgita, for all its emphasis on compassion, peace and love, teaches the warrior to carry out his caste duty of fighting in a spirit of pure detachment, on the grounds that men do not really die, since the self is eternal and indestructible. Admittedly modern Hindu interpreters treat this first part of the Bhagavadgita as allegorical, and as referring to the war of good against evil, in much the same way as C. S. Lewis suggested that the 'enemies' in the Psalms should be thought of as our sins.[11] But in neither case is the problem overcome – neither that of the psalmist's vindictiveness, nor that of the amoral nature of the mystic's concentration.

The problem of comparative religious ethics has been illustrated here by examples from the religious traditions of India. There is clearly a great deal of work to be done before fair and just comparisons can be made. Similarly careful comparison needs to be made in the important case of Islam. It was quite unfair of Troeltsch to dismiss Islam, ethically speaking, as a religion of law, despite the fact that, unlike the Hindu renaissance, the recent revival of Islam has taken a sharply legalistic form in countries such as Iran and Pakistan. But the inner spirit of Muslim ethics is captured much more pertinently by the story told by Wilfred Cantwell Smith[12] about his coming upon on old Muslim fruit-seller in the Himalayas, selling oranges by weight and using three small stones to weigh out a sīr (two pounds) of oranges. There was no way of checking the fruit-seller's honesty, but Cantwell Smith had no hesitation in believing him when he said that the verse from the Qur'an, 'Lo! He over all things is watching', was always ringing in his ears. This simple tale of transparent honesty fostered by a man's religion, can appear, to an unsympathetic critic, to exemplify an ultimately prudential ethic, just as the Sermon on the Mount can be read in terms, primarily, of reward and punishment. But in neither case is a religiously motivated ethic properly construed in prudential terms. In both cases the virtues fostered by belief in God are better construed as a matter of religious response and gratitude.

Further examination of Islam's capacity to sustain an adequate ethic would focus again on the question of social adequacy and the Muslim conception of social justice. This cannot be undertaken here.

All the great religions of the world, despite their differences, have some claim, at their best, to be fostering love and compassion, service of the neighbour and a concern for the right ordering of society. However stagnant they may have become at certain stages in their history, they can and do undergo renaissance and reform and become again the vehicles of human good. How should exponents of Christian ethics view these facts? On both human and theological grounds, it seems that they should welcome these facts as signs of the universal Spirit of God at work in human religion, just as it was argued in chapter one that such signs should be welcomed in human nature and relationships as such. The ability of the religions to foster goodness and love, like the capacity of secular men and women to manifest the virtues, should, for Christians, be an indication that the God revealed in Christ is God of the whole world, the source of all value as of all being. Doubtless, the character of Christ will exercise, for Christians, a normative role in their detection and appreciation of this activity of the Spirit outside the Covenant, just as it exercises a normative role in their own self-criticism as individuals and as a Church. But clearly, just as empirical

Christianity may be convicted of inadequacy by Marxist social concern, empirical Christianity may be convicted of sin by the compassion of the Buddhist saint. On his own admission, the Christian missionary, C. F. Andrews, learned much of what it meant to be a Christian from the Hindu, Gandhi.

NOTES

1. H. Kraemer, *The Christian Message in a Non-Christian World*, p. 86. For Kraemer's views on tolerance, see above p. 80.
2. F. Schleiermacher, *The Christian Faith* (English trans., Edinburgh: T. & T. Clark, 1928), pp. 34–39.
3. E. Troeltsch, *The Absoluteness of Christianity* (English trans., London: SCM Press, 1972, pp. 107–116.
4. R. Niebuhr, *An Interpretation of Christian Ethics*, p. 81.
5. A. C. Danto, *Mysticism and Morality* (New York: Basic Books, 1972, and Harmondsworth: Penguin Books, 1976).
6. See J. A. T. Robinson, *In the End, God* (London: James Clarke, 1950) p. 123.
7. Quoted from J. W. Bowker, *Problems of Suffering in the Religions of the World* (Cambridge University Press, 1970).
8. N. Smart, *A Dialogue of Religions* (London: SCM Press, 1960), chapter VII.
9. London: Collins, 1974.
10. Katha Upanishad, 2. 19.
11. C. S. Lewis, *Reflections on the Psalms* (London: Bles, 1958).
12. W. Cantwell Smith, *Questions of Religious Truth* (London: Gollancz, 1967).

CHAPTER SEVEN

The Place of Ethics in the Christian Religion

One of the problems which emerged from the brief excursion into the field of comparative religion in the last chapter was the tendency in some strands of Eastern religion to speak of a transcending of good and evil, in which ethical distinctions disappear. But it now needs to be asked whether Christianity too does not relativise the ethical, at least to the extent of speaking of other values as needing equal recognition, but perhaps speaking even of higher values too.

It is indeed possible to paint an over-moralistic picture of human life. There is an excellent passage in Bonhoeffer's *Ethics*, cautioning against this error.[1] Bonhoeffer points out that man is not at every moment of his life confronted with final choices between good and evil, or with the necessity of fulfilling some higher purpose. A finite human existence includes times for eating and drinking as well as for deliberate action, times for rest and play as well as for earnest endeavour. There is, of course, an ethical dimension to life. Man is a morally responsible being. But 'the ethical phenomenon . . . is fundamentally misunderstood if the unconditional character of the experience of obligation is taken to imply an exclusive and all-embracing claim. To understand it in this way is to injure and destroy the creaturely wholeness of life'.

115

This sane and balanced view constitutes a standing refutation of both secular and Christian moralism, and shows a maturity of judgement that falsifies any easy Freudian dismissal of religious people as inevitably immature. For Bonhoeffer, the will of God includes not only the specifically moral values but other realms and dimensions of life as well. They all constitute what he calls 'creaturely wholeness'.

Among the elements mentioned by Bonhoeffer as requiring time and as helping to constitute this 'creaturely wholeness' was *play*. Much might be said about the significance and inportance of play in human life; but it is remarkable that the sociologist, Peter Berger, should include the phenomenon of play among his so-called 'signals of transcendence' – aspects of man's being that point beyond the ordinary everyday world to the possibility of a transcendent dimension.[2] Berger stresses the timeless quality of play. He quotes Nietzsche: 'All joy wills eternity – wills deep, deep eternity.' In fact it seems that Zarathustra, on whose lips these words are placed, was meant by Nietzsche to be referring to eternal recurrence.[3] But this does not necessarily invalidate Berger's suggestion that play is one of the self-transcending factors in human existence. If so, this is a reminder that it is not only the moral dimension that provides a springboard for theistic faith.

There is no question, in this high evaluation of the place of play in human life, of its encroaching on the ethical dimension. Still less is there any transcending of the ethical in the sense that disturbed the critic of eastern mystical religion.

Comparison might be drawn with the even higher place of play in Hindu mythology. There is the divine dance in which the god Shiva brings the world into being. There is Krishna's amorous play with the cow-girls, that forms a much loved

116

element in Vaishnavite folk-lore. But in both these cases, conflict with the ethical seems to arise.

From play, we pass on to consider art and aesthetic values in general. Ever since Plato's *Symposium* 'the beautiful' has been subject to philosophical scrutiny. In the Middle Ages, 'pulchrum' ('beautiful'), like 'ens', 'unum', 'bonum' and 'verum' ('being', 'one', 'good' and 'true') was regarded as one of the 'transcendentals' – the most general and all-pervasive features of reality – of God's reality as well as that of creatures. In more recent philosophy, by contrast, aesthetic theory has tended to emphasise the subjective pole of our delight in beautiful objects, and, in any case, to treat the beautiful as a more restricted range of aesthetically pleasing objects and states of affairs. Nevertheless the contemplation of beautiful objects has widely been regarded as an end in itself, an intrinsic value, as it was by G. E. Moore.[5]

It is not very difficult for the Christian religion to baptise the notion of the beautiful and indeed to see it as a pointer to theistic faith. The doctrine of creation involves seeing the world of nature as God's handiwork and the beauty of nature is often thought of as revelatory of the mind of God. Equally, human creativity in all the forms of art can be seen as a participation in and reflection of the divine creativity – part of the image of God in man. Nor need any of this conflict with the ethical, though there is the danger of resorting to a totally aesthetic attitude to life or of failing to let the claims of the ethical carry their weight in relation to those of the aesthetic. The temptation of the artist is to let the claims of his art and of his own integrity as an artist override the just claims of his family or his neighbour.

One of the criticisms of Christian ethics made by Blanshard concerned its relative neglect of aesthetic values. Against this criticism may be set the theology of the Swiss Roman Catholic theologian, Hans Urs von Balthasar (b. 1905).[6] Von Balthasar goes right back to the medieval treatment of beauty as one of the fundamental determinations of being, and insists that it should be as central a dimension for religion and theology as truth and goodness. Reality, indeed, on this ancient view, manifests itself as beautiful. Beauty is of the very stuff of being. In the first of the two articles referred to in the last footnote, J. K. Riches spells out the implications of this view as follows: 'if beauty is a fundamental determination of being, and as such bound up with truth and goodness, then it follows that truth without beauty loses its power of conviction, goodness without beauty leads to a chilly, charmless moralism, beauty without goodness and truth either falls into a sterile aestheticism or falls victim to the demonic'. There can, on this view, be no ultimate clash between beauty, truth and goodness. What von Balthasar brings out is the beauty of the divine love and its presence in our midst. But there is no denying the paradoxical nature of this beauty. The beauty of the divine love, its glory (Herrlichkeit) is most profoundly seen in the cross of Christ by which mankind is redeemed. We contemplate the wonder of the divine love as we contemplate and share in the cross. So there can be no question of the contemplative, aesthetic aspect being prized apart from the active ethical aspect of reality. This is an example of how the actual content of a Christian mystical experience resists the bifurcation between the contemplative and the practical that has troubled critics of eastern mysticism.

Such a treatment of truth, goodness and beauty in fundamental theology is a very interesting one, not least when set against Blanshard's and Kaufmann's criticism of Christianity for its failure to do justice to the claims of truth and beauty.

But it might be thought that von Balthasar's unified vision of truth, goodness and beauty in God's creative and redemptive work is achieved at the cost of too great a reliance on medieval philosophy. For this reason, Bonhoeffer's more down to earth theology might be preferred. Bonhoeffer, it will be recalled, simply insisted that there be a time for play as well as earnest endeavour, for joy as well as renunciation.

It is instructive to compare both writers with a third, the English moral philosopher and theologian, Hastings Rashdall (1858–1924).[7] Rashdall was very much concerned to stress the ethical nature of the Christian religion and at times appears to reduce the first of the two great commandments to the second; love of God, it seems, can only be shown in love of the neighbour. An over-moralising of religion of the kind criticised by Bonhoeffer may be suspected in Rashdall's case. Certainly, in his chapter, entitled, 'Is Religion Wholly Ethical?', Rashdall shows himself strongly opposed to the idea that 'the religious attitude carries us into some super-moral region and enables us to attain a point of view from which moral distinctions are transcended'. Any hint of such transcendence, such as we found in certain strands of Indian mysticism, would be rejected categorically by Rashdall. He continues, however, by admitting that 'even those who believe in a Morality which is in essential harmony with Religion, and in a Religion which does not seek to transcend Morality may possibly object to our limiting the contents of the religious consciousness entirely to the moral ideal.' This would appear to be Bonhoeffer's point. Rashdall attempts to meet it by widening the conception of the moral to include, though as subordinate elements, the right appreciation of nature and beauty in scientific knowledge and art. Similarly, he allows a place for worship, not so much as an end in itself but as a

119

means to that knowledge of God, out of which the moral life flows. To be fair to Rashdall, we should note his qualification of this position. He goes on to say that worship, like intellectual and aesthetic culture 'is both a means and an end – a means to the ideal life of the soul but also one of those activities in which that life consists.' The pursuit of truth and beauty are to be subordinated to the love of our fellow-men, but that love includes the desire 'to promote for them a good which includes the love of truth and beauty'. 'Only when thus subordinated do they form elements in the love of God, and become part of the end which worship promotes, and of which in a sense it forms a part.'

We find, then, here a third way of accommodating other values than the moral into a unified conception of religion and value. For Bonhoeffer it was a matter of allowing a place for different values and activities; for von Balthasar, it was a matter of achieving a unified ontology of beauty, goodness and truth; for Rashdall, it was a matter of widening the conception of the ethical to include beauty, truth and worship in a love of God showing itself in love of the neighbour. For none of these writers are the claims of the ethical overridden by those of other values.

In considering Rashdall's views, we have moved on from the question of aesthetic and intellectual values to the purely religious sphere of worship; and indeed for von Balthasar, the 'aesthetic' includes religious contemplation. It is at this point that the critic of Christianity may feel that the ethical is most in danger of being relativised and transcended. Rashdall's opposition to such transcendence is quite clear, but the question remains whether he has captured the essence of Christianity on the matter, or whether Christianity envisages situations in which the claims of God take precedence over the claims of duty. It is at this point that we come up against the special considerations affecting the ethics of vocation. We have already touched on this in referring to the danger of the subordination of ethical claims to those of the artist's or musician's vocation. The problem is seen most acutely in the case of a man who feels that he is called to devote his life to contemplative prayer.

Here we need something of the mature wisdom of Bonhoeffer in insisting not only that there are times for different values and activities, but also that there are special vocations to 'the religious life' as well as to the life of art or scholarship. Not every man is called to devote his life to social and political activity to the same degree. The ministry of Jesus himself exemplifies the subordination of family and political concern to the claims of his special and unique mission. On the other hand, the ministry of Jesus both in word and deed, is paradigmatic of the way in which the needs of the neighbour are to be met. There was no question of the subordination of the ethical.

This problem of whether, in Christianity, the religious can ever be held to transcend the ethical was brought to most acute expression in the writings of the Danish philosopher, Søren Kierkegaard (1813–1855).

As is well known, the dominant theme of Kierkegaard's philosophy is that of choice or decision. In his book, *Either/ Or* (1843), he presses upon the reader the necessity of choice between two ways of life, which he calls 'the aesthetic' and 'the ethical'. It is clear from his description, in the first half of the book, of the man who lives only in the realm of the aesthetic, that he is thinking of aestheticism in a pejorative sense, of the man who has succumbed to the life of sophisticated hedonism. By contrast, the second half of the book presents us with the man who has opted to live on the ethical plane, in the sphere of duties and demands. The book is clearly autobiographical and portrays a moment of discontinuity in Kierkegaard's own life. The theme of the necessity of choice between sharply posed alternatives may be illustrated by two short quotations:

'Every aesthetic view of life is despair, it was said. This was attributed to the fact that it was built upon what may be and may not be. Such is not the case with the ethical view of life, for it builds upon what essentially belongs to being. The aesthetical, it was said, is that in a man whereby he immediately is the man he is, the ethical is that whereby a man becomes what he becomes.'[8]

'He who chooses himself ethically has himself as his task, and not as a possibility merely, not as a toy to be played with arbitrarily. He can choose himself ethically only when he chooses himself in continuity and so has himself as a task that is manifoldly defined.'[9]

There is a great deal to be said in favour of this existentialist picture of a man's life as a task to be undertaken, though it is, no doubt, in some danger of that over-moralising of human life, about which Bonhoeffer warned. And Kierkegaard's insistence on exclusive choice is undoubtedly extreme. We notice in this presentation of the aesthetic and the ethical as stark alternatives no discussion of the place of other values in an ethically orientated life, nor of the elements of ethical sensibility in an aesthetically orientated life. Nevertheless, it is easier to follow Kierkegaard here, where he draws the line between the aesthetic and the ethical than it is to follow him when he goes on to draw a line between the ethical and the religious (or Christian, since he never considers other religions). This is the aspect of Kierkegaard's thought on which we shall need to concentrate.

The book, *Fear and Trembling* (1843), opens with some vivid narratives, re-telling the story of Abraham and Isaac. In one of them, Abraham turns on the boy and seizes him by the throat and throws him to the ground and says, 'Stupid boy, dost thou then suppose that I am thy father? I am an idolator. Dost thou suppose that this is God's bidding? No, it is my desire.' Isaac trembles and cried out, 'O God in heaven, have compassion upon me . . . If I have no father upon earth, be Thou my father!' Abraham says in a low voice to himself, 'O Lord in heaven, I thank Thee. After all, it is better for him to believe that I am a monster, rather than that he should lose his faith in Thee.'[10]

To the modern consciousness, the story of Abraham and Isaac in the book of Genesis is a morally offensive tale. It is explained by biblical critics as an aetiological myth, justifying the abolition of child sacrifice, and held to have no particular significance for faith today. But Kierkegaard does not re-tell the story in this fashion in order to bring out its moral enormity. On the contrary, he launches into a panegyric upon Abraham, as a paradigm of faith, whose faith and obedience were such that 'he arose and took his son and went to the land of Moriah to offer up his son', notwithstanding the ethically preposterous nature of the supposed divine command. Kierkegaard uses this story to illustrate what he calls the 'teleological suspension of the ethical' – that is to say, the fact, as Kierkegaard supposes it to be, that, in religion, a man must not hold back from the 'leap of faith' even when ethical norms would unquestionably be flouted. Faith is a higher category. Its teleology is such that even the ethical may be suspended.

The logic of this view is spelled out in a section entitled

'problem I: Is there such a thing as a teleological suspension of the ethical?' The ethical, Kierkegaard asserts, is the universal, applying to everyone, and the question at issue is whether the universal is the highest category or whether the individual in faith is called to rise above the universal and indeed assert himself against it. Kierkegaard's answer is that the relation to God in which Abraham stood did indeed lift him above the universal duty of a father to his son.[11]

How are we to evaluate this remarkable conviction of the possibility, in religion, of a teleological suspension of the ethical? The considerations advanced in this book should lead us to reject it. If human nature, human goodness, human relationships and human solidarity do, in fact, provide some indication of the nature and the will of God the Creator, sufficient to constitute the basis of moral criticism of purported revelation claims, then, whatever further insight or enhancement be given in revelation through the character of Christ and the experience of Christian discipleship and Christian community, it cannot flatly contradict the ethical or suspend it. That would be to assert self-contradiction in God. The will of God in grace cannot annul the will of God in creation. Unless the religious demand can be recognised as morally credible, it cannot be accepted as genuine. In other words, our conviction of the divine command must be tested by moral criteria, even if our moral vision is itself enlarged in the process. Morality may be enhanced, but it cannot be abrogated. It is always less certain that a purported divine command in fact has its source in God than that the claims of morality should be respected. To that extent, Rashdall's insistence on the primacy of the ethical must be acknowledged as correct.

But there remains a point in Kierkegaard's suspicion of the

universal. If the ethical prescribes the general form of moral life, there is more to be said about the particular forms of individual and common life to which men and women should aspire. (Kierkegaard, it should be noted, was wrong to lay his whole stress on the individual.) Our own guarded defence of situation ethics bore this out with regard to the ethical itself, in both its individual and social aspects; for we cannot say in advance what the particular situation will require of love in action. We recall Bonhoeffer's insistence that conformity to Christ is a matter of the actual particular relationships between believers and their Lord. In this chapter we have seen that other values than the ethical also have their place in human life, not least the individual's vocation. But again there can be no question of the suspension of the ethical. Any argument to that effect is self-deception, and invites the moral protest of secular ethics, appealing to our common humanity.

In summary, the place of ethics in the Christian religion is this: moral values and the claims of duty are not the only values and needs in God's world. We have briefly considered a range of values, from those of rest and play, through those of truth and beauty, to those of worship, contemplation and special vocation. None of these can override the claims of the good. Morality, in both its individual and social forms, cannot be suspended. But we have also seen that human life, in its non-ethical as in its ethical aspects, is enhanced and inspired to further ideals of life through the revelation of God in Christ, and through living participation in the Body of Christ. Christian life embraces the love of truth and beauty, as well as the love of God and the neighbour.

NOTES

1. D. Bonhoeffer, *Ethics*, Fontana edition, pp. 264 f.
2. P. Berger, *A Rumour of Angels* (Harmondsworth: Penguin Books 1970).
3. See above p. 25.
4. Vaishnavites are worshippers of Vishnu, whose 'avatar' (incarnation) Krinshna is.
5. G. E. Moore, *Principia Ethica*, chapter VI.
6. Von Balthasar's major work, *Herrlichkeit*, is only now in process of translation. A good, short, example of his work is *Love Alone the Way of Revelation* (English trans., London: Burns and Oates, 1968). See also J. K. Riches, 'The Theology of Hans Urs von Balthasar' in *Theology* for November and December 1972.
7. H. Rashdall, *The Theory of Good and Evil* (Oxford University Press, 1907), especially Book III, chapter two.
8. S. Kierkegaard, *Either/Or* (Eng. trans., London: OUP, 1944) Vol. II, p. 189.
9. op. cit. p. 216.
10. S. Kierkegaard, *Fear and Trembling* (Eng., Anchor Books ed., New York: Doubleday, 1954, Prelude I, p. 27.
11. op. cit., pp. 64–77. On Kierkegaard, see further W. Lowrie, *Kierkegaard* (Oxford University Press, 1938) and H. Blackham, *Six Existentialist Thinkers* (London: Routledge and Kegan Paul, 1952).

CHAPTER EIGHT

A Positive Interpretation of Christian Ethics

This book has been chiefly concerned with criticisms of Christian ethics and how those criticisms might be met. We have seen that the recurring stock objections that have been made against Christian ethics since the time of the Enlightenment are largely based on misunderstandings. Christianity does not, in essence, teach an ethic of reward and punishment. Rather it commends an utterly disinterested love. Christianity does not subject men and women to an alien authority. Rather it respects men's freedom and responsibility within an overall structure of dependence on God as the source of all men's good. It fosters human growth into mature moral agency in the context of a developing spiritual relation to God. Christianity does not restrict its ethical scope to the individual and his perfection. Rather it insists on spelling out the will of God in terms of social justice as well as of individual goodness. Christianity does not claim exclusive ethical insight. Rather its own aberrations, past and present, invite criticism in the face not only of its own ideal, but also of our common humanity, which Christianity sees as itself reflecting the divine goodness. Moreover we have seen how other religions too contain resources for the fostering and sustaining of compassion and love of the neighbour. This fact can be recognised

127

by Christians as indicative of the presence and activity of the same Spirit which they know as the Spirit of Christ. We have seen too that a mature Christian ethic can leave room for other values, such as truth and beauty, and indeed encourage contemplation as well as action, special vocation as well as moral responsibility. But in no way can Christianity countenance a transcending of morality. Christianity and ethics are inseparable.

The adequacy of Christian ethics, however, cannot be established simply by answering criticism. Certainly the objections need to be met. But once the misunderstandings have been cleared away and the alternatives themselves examined critically, we need to consider the more fundamental question whether the Christian ethic can claim adequacy in the sense of meeting all the fundamental needs and aspirations of humanity and providing a vision and resources sufficient for the realisation of the highest possible individual and communal ideal. In this final chapter, therefore, an attempt is made to set out, positively, though inevitably in schematic form, an interpretation of the fundamental content of a specifically Christian ethic.

But before we leave the topic of secular and non-Christian religious ethics, we need to reflect on what Christians have to learn from their critics. So far we have accorded positive significance to secular ethics as reflecting the will of God in creation, manifested in our common humanity, and to the ethics of other religions as reflecting the hidden presence of the Spirit of the same Christ who manifests the nature and the will of God openly in his incarnate life and in the witness of those who have consciously accepted that revelation. It seems that the most that secular or non-Christian religious ethics can do is mediate something of the will of God for man to those outside the sphere of Christian faith and act as sources of valid moral criticism where empirical Christianity has lost its ethical bearings. This is not a negative view of non-Christian ethics and it certainly enables Christians to accord to other manifestations of human goodness and social progress a positive role in the providence of God. But it does not seem to allow the Christian individual or the Christian Church to learn something creative and new from non-Christian ethics, something that could not be learned from specifically Christian ethics, properly understood.

If this is our conclusion on the nature and function of non-Christian ethics, we may have progressed beyond the negative depreciatory attitudes of earlier Christian generations, but we have not done justice to the actual qualities of human goodness and social idealism that are found outside the sphere of Christian ethics, and we have not begun to take the measure of the confession of C. F. Andrews, mentioned at the end of chapter six, that he had learned much of what it meant to be a Christian from the Hindu, Gandhi. It is perfectly true that ethical ideals which turn out to be actively opposed to Christ and to the revelation of God's nature and will which he brought – the ethical doctrines of Nietzsche, for example – can only be rejected by Christians as false to the nature of man as God intended him to be. But there is a great deal of profound moral worth in the lives of non-Christian individuals from Socrates to Gandhi and in the teachings of non-Christian moralists from Aristotle to Marx (to say nothing of contemporary examples) that is not only quite compatible with Christ and his revelation but which reveals new facets of human goodness and human idealism, from which Christians can only learn with gratitude. Such human goodness and such human idealism can be regarded as less or more conscious reflections, in different social and cultural environments, of the goodness of God the Creator. Christians may certainly learn something new of the many-faceted image of God in man from human goodness outside the covenant of grace.

This is to apply to the sphere of ethics what has been said more generally about divine revelation in other religions by, among others, Geoffrey Parrinder, in answer to the question, put deliberately to Christians, 'Is the Bhagavad-Gita the Word of God?'.[1] Parrinder's answer to this question is first that Christians can certainly accept the revelatory, indeed salvific, nature of this Hindu scripture, insofar as it accords with Christ, but further, that Christians can learn something new of God's ways with men in other cultures in any such religious form of expression, provided that what was revealed in Christ is not contradicted. Similarly we may say that wherever moral goodness and social justice are to be found, in forms compatible with God's final self-revelation in Christ, there is to be discerned the hidden presence and activity of this same God. To put the point concisely and more positively: the Christian should want and hope to know what forms of goodness God has evoked in the millions who live or have lived outside the sphere of Christian revelation.

Such recognition of new and creative moral life and vision 'outside the covenant' may be acknowledged without denying the perversions and corruptions to which any human form of life, including the Christian, is subject, and without denying the normative and final revelation of God's will for man, which Christians believe is there to be discerned in Christ. Christ, properly understood, remains the final key for human knowledge of God's will, and that is why C. F. Andrews said that Gandhi's example taught him much of what it meant to be a *Christian*. The point is that conformity to God's nature and will *is*, ultimately speaking, conformity to Christ, whether it be explicit or implicit. Implicit conformity to Christ may open our eyes to something of what it means to be a Christian, but in the end of the day it is Christ to whom all men and women are to be conformed. Consequently it is an indispensable aspect of Christian belief to hold that Christ himself is the criterion of all good, and that implicit response to God in Christ will one day be transformed into explicit response.

The Christian ideal, that is to say, cannot be regarded simply as one of many equally valid options open to mankind. In an influential article,[2] P. F. Strawson has argued that, while a common social morality is necessary and obligatory for all men, individual ideals of life, over and above that common social morality are various and optional, and that there is value in the range of choice. This characteristically liberal view is not open to Christianity, which is bound to see God's self-revelation in Christ as possessing normative and universal scope.

The question remains, What is the specific contribution of Christian ethics? What is it that God's self-disclosure in Jesus Christ, properly understood, reveals and makes possible for men and women, both individually and communally, as a normative and universal ideal? This question is not easy to answer in plain words. If we could succeed in stating satisfactorily the positive content of Christian ethics once and for all, we should have achieved more than any of the representatives of Christian ethics whom we have reviewed in the course of this book. No one statement which we have considered proved free of some imbalance. Kirk's conception of the vision of God failed to bring out the social dimension of Christian ethics adequately. Barth's theological 'actualism' failed to do justice to the doctrine of Creation and the image of God in man. Bonhoeffer's conception of 'conformity to Christ' did not prevent him from idiosyncracies of judgement in concrete cases. Niebuhr's interpretation of love as justice failed to reckon adequately with the Christian doctrine of redemption. Situation ethics failed to grasp the structure of morality and the accumulated wisdom of human moral experience. Liberation theology was in danger of succumbing to Marxist social revolution at the expense of personal values. Nevertheless the positive insights of all these authors and schools will doubtless find a place in our own attempt to set down, in summary form, the content of Christian ethics.

Quite apart from the tendency of individual authors and particular schools to stress one aspect of the Christian ethic to the neglect of others, there is a perfectly good reason why the actual content of Christian ethics should have proved so hard to characterise, a reason which all our authors and schools have themselves been aware of to a greater or lesser extent. It is that Christian ethics speaks of the good for man in terms of particular living relations between Christ and his followers. There are, as we shall see, certain general features of a Christ-like life, and of a Spirit-filled community. Conformity to Christ has indeed a content and a structure, specifiable in general terms. Moreover the life of Christ himself, being the life of God incarnate here on earth, is thought of in Christian ethics as paradigmatic. The imitation of Christ is an indispensable aspect of the Christian ideal. But the inmost content of Christian ethics cannot be fully captured in general terms, nor even in the particular example of Jesus. Christian moral life, in both its individual and social dimensions, is also the product of an actual relation to the living Spirit of God and of Christ, peculiar to each individual, each group and each situation. The notion of the imitation of Christ has its limitations, therefore, even for Christian ethics; for we cannot ignore the special vocation of Jesus himself and the particular context and culture in which he lived. The universal significance of Christ for all men and in all contexts is not simply to be deduced by meditation on his incarnate life; rather the mind of Christ is discerned through participation in the Body of the risen Christ in each and every context. This flexibility is an essential aspect of the adequacy of Christian ethics. As G. F. Woods emphasised in his writings on Christian ethics,[3] it is the personal nature of the Christian moral standard, in the sense not only of a real exemplary life, but also of the personal relation between God, as the source of all good, and his creatures in their various cultural and historical situations that constitutes the heart of Christian morality. Indeed it can be argued that only such a personal moral standard has the flexibility to prescribe and inspire the good in any and every human condition.

For all that, something must be said here of the general character of Christian ethics. If we go back to the New Testament beginnings, we find in the letters of Paul, John and other leaders of the early Church, a delineation of certain fundamental attitudes and qualities of life that are to be fostered in the nascent Christian communities, qualities, indeed, which are recognised as being, ideally, natural products of response to the Christian gospel and participation in the Christian Church. Certainly they reflect both the teaching and example of Jesus himself, especially the manner in which he trod the way of the Cross, but they are also held to manifest the active grace of Christ in the lives of his followers. These attitudes are spelled out in Paul's list of the fruits of the Spirit: love, joy, peace, patience, kindness, goodness, faithfulness, gentleness, self-control.[4] Already in Paul's great hymn to love,[5] we see the basic principle of love, including love of the enemy, emerging as the ultimate criterion of human life and action, just because it is held to mirror the love of God revealed in Christ and indeed to *be* that love in action in and through the lives of Christians. The same criterion is urged in the letters of John.[6] We also see the beginnings – though only the beginnings – of Christian attempts to discover the mind of Christ in respect of problems of social life, such as poverty and riches, power and violence.[7] The history of Christian ethics is the history of reflection on the innumerable attempts, both individual and corporate, to apply the ultimate principle and the characteristic attitudes, discernible in the way of Christ, to the various needs of men and women in their particular historical circumstances. A vast amount of practical wisdom and a vast amount of ethical theory have been accumulated down the Christian centuries, giving structure and shape to the search for authentic Christian life amidst the needs and pressures of very different cultures and times. We have briefly looked at a number of recent and contemporary examples of the fruits of this long search. Sometimes the emphasis has been on spiritual growth into a vision of God that inspires heroic acts of sacrificial love. Sometimes the emphasis has been on the struggle for justice and commitment to work for the time when no one rests content while his neighbour is in need.

At this point we may pause for final reflection on the problem of the relation between the individual and the social dimensions to which we have repeatedly drawn attention in the course of this book. Christianity certainly addresses itself to individuals. It is individuals who hear its message and allow themselves to be transformed into instruments of the divine love. But that love cannot be a question simply of immediate inter-personal relations. Nor can its social expression be restricted to the Christian fellowship itself. We have seen how love of the neighbour necessarily finds expression in commitment to the struggle for justice. Only in the end will Christian community and humanity coincide. In the present stage of God's creative process which we call the history of the world, the adequacy of Christian ethics rests in part on its ability to inspire men and women to establish a just framework for human life on earth – for all human beings, whether or not they call themselves Christians. I deliberately refer to a just *framework*; for Christian ethics does not make the mistake of idolising the state as such. Rather it sees the justly ordered state as only a framework within which human beings may pursue their goals and realise their ideals, including that of true community.[8] But political effort towards ensuring that the framework is just is an inalienable Christian obligation, if love of the neighbour is to be taken seriously.

To return to our general summary: ethics, as such, is a theoretical discipline, and we have concentrated, in this study, on the problem of the theoretical adequacy of Christian ethics. But the subject matter of Christian ethics is human goodness and human community, as the lives of men and women are in fact conformed to Christ through the working of his Spirit. The proof of the theory lies in the practice. A study of the practical adequacy of Christians ethics would be a study of actual Christian lives, of saints and social reformers, of men and women who have shown the love of Christ in their protest at injustice and in caring for the poor, the sick and the dying, often in situations of utter hopelessness, at least by any purely human standard. It would be a study of the transformation of situations of oppression and the manifestation in every context of authentic forms of human brotherhood and community.

On the theoretical plane, however, it may be said in conclusion that the ultimate basis for the claim to adequacy on ths part of Christian ethics is the fact that the love of which it speaks is, in reality, the source and goal of all there is. The 'Love that moves the sun and the other stars'[9] is the ultimate source of all created being and value. Human goodness in all its multifarious individual and social forms already reflects something of the nature and will of that creative source. That love is revealed concretely and specifically in the life and teaching and in the passion and cross of Christ. Conformity to Christ is therefore conformity to the divine love. Spiritual resources, the divine forgiveness and the immanent grace of the Holy Spirit of God, are given to men and women through the religions of the world and particularly through the spiritual and sacramental presence and activity of the risen Christ. But those resources do not compel. The living Christ awakens and inspires men and women to mature reflection and responsible action, in both inter-personal and social life. From this vast field of spiritual relations stems the variety and fecundity of authentic Christian existence and commitment. But just because the human response is free, the scope for error and inadequacy both in theory and in practice is great. As was said at the beginning of chapter four, no single presentation of Christian ethics can claim final adequacy, and, apart from Christ himself, no concrete realisation of the Christian ideal, in individual or in communal life, can claim final adequacy. Only in Christ and in the end, when God is all in all, is the gap between the ideal and the real fully closed and the divine goodness and love perfectly mirrored in creaturely goodness and love. The time for theory will then be past. In the mean-time, when Christians speak of the adequacy of Christian ethics, they speak of an ideal – the ideal of conformity to the one who brought the mind and heart of the love behind the universe into our midst, and of the spiritual resources for the eventual realisation of that ideal.

NOTES

1. See J. Hick (ed.), *Truth and Dialogue* (London: Sheldon Press, 1974). Parrinder is deliberately echoing W. Cantwell Smith's chapter title, 'Is the Qur'an the Word of God?', in his book, *Questions of Religious Truth* (London: Gollancz, 1967).
2. 'Social Morality and Individual Ideal', *Philosophy* XXXVI, 1961, reprinted in *Freedom and Resentment* (London: Methuen, 1974).
3. *Theological Explanation* (Welwyn: James Nisbet, 1958), chapter XVII, and *A Defence of Theological Ethics* (Cambridge University Press, 1966).
4. Galatians 5.22
5. I Corinithians 13.
6. I John 4.7–21.
7. A fresh assessment of these topics is to be found in the short studies by the Tübingen New Testament scholar. Martin Hengel. See *Property and Riches in the Early Church* (Eng. trans., London: SCM Press, 1974), *Victory over Violence* (Eng. trans., London: SPCK, 1975), and *Christ and Power* (Eng. trans., Belfast: Christian Journals, 1977). On the fundamental qualities of life envisaged as ideal in early Christian ethics as well as on their relation to the Christian gospel of salvation, see C. H. Dodd, *Gospel and Law* (Cambridge University Press, 1951).
8. It will be recalled that this was Bonhoeffer's view. See p. 99 above.
9. Dante, *Paradiso*, Canto XXXIII, line 145.

Select Bibliography

(in addition to works cited in the text and notes)

P. R. Baelz, *Ethics and Belief* (London: Sheldon Press, 1977)

P. T. Geach, *The Virtues* (Cambridge University Press, 1977)

J. M. Gustafson, *Can Ethics be Christian?* (University of Chicago Press, 1975)

B. Häring, *Morality is for Persons* (London: Vision Press, 1972)

A. Kee (ed.), *A Reader in Political Theology* (London: SCM Press, 197)

B. G. Mitchell, *Morality: Religious and Secular* (Oxford: The Clarendon Press, 1980)

P. Ramsey, *Basic Christian Ethics* (London: SCM Press, 1953)

N. G. H. Robinson, *The Groundwork of Christian Ethics* (London: Collins, 1971)

A. R. Vidler (ed.), *Objections to Christian Belief* (London: Constable, 1963)

K. Ward, *Ethics and Christianity* (London: Allen and Unwin, 1970)

Index

141